Editor-in-Chief and Founder:
   Lyndon H. LaRouche, Jr.
Editorial Board: *Lyndon H. LaRouche, Jr. , Helga
   Zepp-LaRouche, Robert Ingraham, Tony
   Papert, Gerald Rose, Dennis Small, Jeffrey
   Steinberg, William Wertz*
Co-Editors: *Robert Ingraham, Tony Papert*
Managing Editor: *Nancy Spannaus*
Technology: *Marsha Freeman*
Books: *Katherine Notley*
Ebooks: *Richard Burden*
Graphics: *Alan Yue*
Photos: *Stuart Lewis*
Circulation Manager: *Stanley Ezrol*

INTELLIGENCE DIRECTORS
Counterintelligence: *Jeffrey Steinberg, Michele
   Steinberg*
Economics: *John Hoefle, Marcia Merry Baker,
   Paul Gallagher*
History: *Anton Chaitkin*
Ibero-America: *Dennis Small*
Russia and Eastern Europe: *Rachel Douglas*
United States: *Debra Freeman*

INTERNATIONAL BUREAUS
Bogotá: *Miriam Redondo*
Berlin: *Rainer Apel*
Copenhagen: *Tom Gillesberg*
Houston: *Harley Schlanger*
Lima: *Sara Madueño*
Melbourne: *Robert Barwick*
Mexico City: *Gerardo Castilleja Chávez*
New Delhi: *Ramtanu Maitra*
Paris: *Christine Bierre*
Stockholm: *Ulf Sandmark*
United Nations, N.Y.C.: *Leni Rubinstein*
Washington, D.C.: *William Jones*
Wiesbaden: *Göran Haglund*

ON THE WEB
e-mail: eirns@larouchepub.com
www.larouchepub.com
www.executiveintelligencereview.com
www.larouchepub.com/eiw
Webmaster: *John Sigerson*
Assistant Webmaster: *George Hollis*
Editor, Arabic-language edition: *Hussein Askary*

EIR (ISSN 0273-6314) *is published weekly
(50 issues), by EIR News Service, Inc.,
P.O. Box 17390, Washington, D.C. 20041-0390.
(703) 777-9451 ext. 415*

European Headquarters: E.I.R. GmbH, Postfach
Bahnstrasse 9a, D-65205, Wiesbaden, Germany
Tel: 49-611-73650
Homepage: http://www.eirna.com
e-mail: eirna@eirna.com
Director: Georg Neudecker

Montreal, Canada: 514-461-1557

Denmark: EIR - Danmark, Sankt Knuds Vej 11,
basement left, DK-1903 Frederiksberg, Denmark.
Tel.: +45 35 43 60 40, Fax: +45 35 43 87 57. e-mail:
eirdk@hotmail.com.

Mexico City: EIR, Sor Juana Inés de la Cruz 242-2
Col. Agricultura C.P. 11360
Delegación M. Hidalgo, México D.F.
Tel. (5525) 5318-2301
eirmexico@gmail.com

Canada Post Publication Sales Agreement
#40683579

Postmaster: Send all address changes to *EIR*, P.O.
Box 17390, Washington, D.C. 20041-0390.

Signed articles in *EIR* represent the views of the
authors, and not necessarily those of the Editorial
Board.

Mankind's Next Breakthrough

EIR Contents

www.larouchepub.com Volume 44, Number 2, January 13, 2017

NASA Photo / Dr. Leonard Weinstein

Cover This Week

Shock waves on breaking the sound barrier: Schlieren photograph of a T-38 at Mach 1.1, altitude 13,700 feet, taken at NASA Wallops in 1993.

MANKIND'S NEXT BREAKTHROUGH

Correction

On page 15, in the Jan. 6, 2017 issue of *EIR*:

The reference to one of 15 Americans addicted to opiates or opioids should have stated that one in 15 Americans are addicted to something (out of 21 million total, the majority of those addicted are alcoholics). About 3 million are addicted to opiates or opioids.

I. Two World Systems at War

Will 2017 See the End of the Euro?

by Claudio Celani

Jan. 10—The incoming Trump Administration should place on their strategic security screens, a highly probable implosion—possibly this year—of the Euro system, and prepare for this eventuality by drafting a set of policies aimed at facilitating an organized transition to a post-Euro system. These policies should include political and financial support for those countries which want to re-establish national sovereignty, consistent with views expressed by the President-elect and his collaborators during and after the U.S. election campaign.

The alternative to such an approach is a mega-bailout of European and Wall Street zombie banks, with a multiple of those trillions of taxpayers' dollars that the Bush and the Obama Administrations spent after 2007-2008.

The most probable candidate for leaving the Euro is Italy. In one way or another, we might have a repetition of 2011, when the European Central Bank (ECB) stopped supporting the Italian sovereign debt; however, this time the Italian establishment won't easily accept further austerity recipes and might decide to leave the Euro system.

Indicative of the widespread sentiment in the country, the daily *Il Sole 24 Ore*, owned by the industrialists' association Confindustria, published a Dec. 30 editorial by its editor-in-chief Roberto Napoletano, who accused the EU institutions of victimizing Italy on the issue of its banking crisis, and stated that "Italian politics cannot accept this Europe."

Three days earlier, Italy's newspaper of record, *Corriere della Sera*, published an op-ed by two economists and former government ministers, Giorgio

CC/Eric Chan
European Central Bank

La Malfa and Paolo Savona, who urged the Italian government to "ask Germany to take the initiative of rethinking the single currency."

The issue at stake is the so-called "Italian banking crisis," which is a result of the protracted decline of the Italian physical economy. Years of EU-imposed austerity policies have caused a serious recession and insolvencies. As a result, Italian banks officially own 200 billion euros of non-performing loans (NPLs), i.e. defaulted loans to companies and families—but the real figure is perhaps double that.

However, the NPL crisis was aggravated by EU regulations themselves (Basel III), which mandate an immediate death sentence for the customer, and the mathematically-certain loss of the loan.

In former times, when a customer was 90 days in default on loans (technically non-performing), the primary task of the bank was to overcome a difficult period together with its customer. Today, if problems arise in a company, the bank must immediately put on the brakes, rate the claims as "at risk," cut further financing, and cover the existing claims with large capital reserves, even if the company has assets.

Thus, *Il Sole* editor Napoletano is right when he says: "Non-performing loans have become the stigma of European banking, and behind that is the steering wheel of an international financial club where Germans and Frenchmen give the orders."

Napoletano accuses the European Banking Authority (EBA), which is part of the ECB, of fixating on the credit side of banks (commercial loans) while at the same time ignoring the leverage factor and the derivatives exposure. The EBA, Napoletano wrote, accepts two things: a leverage of 3%, which was Lehman's leverage, and "another idea, which is deadly, concerning protection of level three assets… thus allowing French and German banks to keep on their balance sheets this sort of 'zombie bank,' without demanding higher capitalization to offset certainly illiquid assets."

Level three assets are assets which have no market, and thus no price. They are worth zero, but banks are allowed to price those assets according to internal models, and put that value on their balance sheet. This is what experts such as FDIC vice-chairman Thomas Hoening have been exposing for a long time, and also what European Parliament member Marco Zanni focused on in his speech at the Schiller Institute in Berlin last year.

Napoletano said:

All the European attention is instead concentrated on NPLs, and of course on Italian NPLs, which are admittedly high but are covered by real collateral, including real estate properties without a speculative bubble,… The result of this dominant thinking is an unbalanced business model, exposed in mid-term financing, where nobody cares about the 'rot' of level three assets and similar garbage, and everyone ends up saying that the European problem is the Italian banks and their NPLs.

Napoletano's attack came after a Dec. 27 meeting between the *Il Sole* editorial board and Italian Finance Minister Gian Carlo Padoan, where Padoan said that "a civil war" was being fought on Italian NPLs.

Padoan, Napoletano wrote, should "take the initiative and challenge a European system… based on shaky fundamentals… Italian politics can no longer accept this Europe, because at the end of this devils' circle, the most probable scenario is that French banks buy Italian banks" and might even swallow Assicurazioni Generali.

In his own way, Napoletano realizes that the world has changed: "Everything changes, Europe does not move: Trump; Brexit; the Pope coming from the end of the world; the comeback of Russia; and a widespread failure of traditional political leaderships to interpret the soul of public opinion, due to reasons that go from elitism to the depth of the economic crisis."

In their op-ed of Dec. 27, Savona and La Malfa went further, demanding that the Euro system be terminated by Germany leaving the Euro. In the alternative, a different system of national currencies should be set up, similar to the Bretton Woods system.

Savona and La Malfa were answering an earlier interview with Clemens Fuest (Dec. 15), head of the Munich-based IFO Institute, who had stated among other things that "If the Euro is an obstacle to growth in Italy, then Italy should leave the Euro."

Along with some inevitable German-bashing, Savona and La Malfa propose the following:

The Italian government should demand, in complete confidentiality, a clarification from Germany, and ask that Germany take the initiative to re-think the single currency. This can happen in one of two ways: the first is that Germany leaves the Euro, reintroducing the D-Mark and letting it float upwards.…

The other is to replace the current mechanism of the single currency with a mechanism of fixed but adjustable exchange-rates, allowing a downsized European Central Bank and the European Investment Bank (EIB) to assume the features of the two Bretton Woods Institutions, the IMF and the World Bank; with the Euro as a reference currency for national currencies (as the Special Drawing Rights were supposed to become), and the EIB working to improve convergence among European countries.

If both options are rejected, then member countries should carry out "fully independent monetary and fiscal policies, and wait and see."

The ECB at War Against Italy

This discussion took place in the aftermath of a decision by the Italian government to bail out Monte dei Paschi di Siena bank (MPS), and a confrontation between Rome, the Frankfurt ECB, and Berlin on whether the bail-out (*de facto* a nationalization) should also include a bail-in, i.e. a confiscation of junior bondholders.

Not only did the ECB and the German government insist that 40,000 retail customers who bought subordinate MPS bonds should be expropriated, but on Dec. 26, the ECB sent a letter to the Monte dei Paschi di Siena Bank, demanding that the bank build a higher capital buffer than previously agreed upon, and raise 8.8 instead of 5 billion in new capital.

In his interview with *Il Sole*, Finance Minister Gian Carlo Padoan did not hide his resentment of this action, which he called "not transparent."

The case of Monte dei Paschi di Siena, the oldest

active bank in the world and a systemic bank, is exemplary of way the EU first destroyed the banking system, and then punished the citizens for its own mistakes.

MPS has a commercial side and an investment side. The MPS crisis was generated first by debt incurred in the investment side, and eventually aggravated by non-performing loans currently amounting to 47 billion euros.

The single major cause of the MPS crisis was its acquisition of Antonveneta Bank in 2008. MPS purchased Antonveneta from Santander at an official price of 9 billion euros, but a total cost of 19 billion euros. To conceal this debt, derivatives contracts were purchased, which increased the debt. It is presumed that MPS was looted in order to bail-out Santander, which was in a precarious situation after having bailed out ABN Amro. In other words, MPS was sacrificed to bail out one part of the bankrupt financial system.

One single person, ECB chairman Mario Draghi, bears responsibility for that. Draghi was the Italian central banker as well as the head of the international Financial Stability Forum. In 2008, he authorized the Antonveneta purchase, even though the supervisory department of the Bank of Italy had warned, one year earlier, that this was a bad deal. Furthermore, Draghi fraudulently authorized the purchase at a "total cost" of 9 billion euros, mixing price with cost.

Today, the same Draghi is pushing MPS to bail in (confiscate) owners of subordinate bonds, those very bonds that he had authorized MPS to issue to cover part of the "costs" of the Antonveneta purchase! Should 40,000 small investors, depositors who were sold those bonds in a fraudulent action, be punished because of mistakes made by Draghi and Co.?

The Italian government has moved to nationalize MPS, and promises not to bail-in those bondholders. The ECB and the German government have signaled that they won't accept that, and insist on a bail-in. If Rome caves in to that, there will be ruinous consequences.

Meanwhile, the elephant in the room has not disappeared, namely Deutsche Bank with its 45 billion euro derivatives portfolio, and other zombie banks which the ECB is keeping alive with an extension of "Quantitative Easing" until the end of the year. This is an unsustainable situation, and if nations want to survive, they should move pre-emptively with a financial reorganization according to Glass-Steagall principles, before the situation explodes in an uncontrolled way.

All the major U.S. banks are exposed to European banks, and vice versa. An explosion of the European banking system means an explosion of the trans-Atlantic system.

The Two Evils

Meanwhile, a second evil has materialized with the publication of the December inflation figures for the Eurozone, which threaten to accelerate the dissolution of the Euro system.

After years of stagnation, inflation has jumped to 1.1% for the Eurozone. However, this is the average between two extremes: whereas Germany with 1.7% is close to the ECB target of 2%, Italy with 0.4% and an annual rate of -0.1% is officially in a deflation.

If the figures for the Eurozone keep rising and approach the German level, the ECB cannot possibly continue its monetary expansion policy, which was motivated by the aim of reaching the 2% inflation target—or better, "below but close to" 2%, as the official ECB mantra has repeated. Representing many in Germany, including mainstream media, Munich-based IFO institute head Clemens Fuest told the *Frankfurter Allgemeine Zeitung* Jan. 4 that "this inflation leap is a signal for ending the expansive money policy of the ECB.... If these figures are confirmed for the Eurozone as a whole, the ECB should terminate the asset purchase program in March 2017."

But if the ECB drops the zero-interest policy and the Assets Purchase Program (APP), this will cause a Eurozone debt crisis, with its epicenter in Italy. Italy must roll over 260 billion of euro debt in 2017, and if the ECB stops purchasing bonds, yields on that debt will skyrocket as in 2011.

Italy has been a master pupil of the EU in the last twenty years, by running a primary surplus each and every year. The price of this is a declining growth in the same period, and the current deflation (-0.1% in 2016). Deflation is a symptom of collapsing demand, and the trend ensures that the debt/GDP ratio will rise.

According to figures released by the Parliamentary Office of the Budget, Italy has paid over 1.7 trillion euros in the last 20 years in interest on its government debt, as much as an entire year of GDP. Of the 260 billion euros of government bonds which Italy is to issue in 2017, 214 billion are to roll over old bonds and 47 billion are to pay interest.

This scenario would add up to the so-called "Italian banking crisis" which we have described above. Faced with this explosive combination and the choice of either submitting to the Troika or leaving the Euro, Italy might easily choose the latter option.

GLASS-STEAGALL

This Is War!

by Robert Ingraham

Jan. 8—On Jan. 3, 2017, as the new 115th Congress convened in Washington, D.C., they were met by an organizing team from the LaRouche Political Action Committee. This team of political activists and volunteers walked the halls of Congress, buttonholed Senators and Congressmen, and took part in numerous meetings, whose primary focus centered on the emergency economic measures which must be taken to save the nation. At the heart of these discussions was the necessity to adopt economic, credit and science policies coherent with Lyndon LaRouche's Four Laws, and, most importantly, the initial urgent action to restore Franklin Roosevelt's Glass-Steagall legislation.

National Archives

Franklin D, Roosevelt signs Glass-Steagall Act, 1933.

protecting our economy from another unnecessary market crash and recession like the one experienced in December of 2007. As you take office, the conditions for a collapse are too similar to those of 2007: rising asset values together with a lack of separation between FDIC-insured banking and risk-investment brokering.

This demand to reinstate Glass-Steagall has now been given an additional grass-roots boost, in the form of two initiatives which have come out of the American Midwest. In Ohio, a group of Democrats, who are calling themselves "Our Revolution," are now circulating a letter and petition calling on President-elect Trump to demand Glass-Steagall restoration in his inaugural and State of the Union addresses. Their call is titled, "Let Us Hold President Donald Trump to his Word: Endorse the Glass-Steagall Act in Your State of the Union Address!" Their petition, addressed to "any and all—Our Revolution, Tea Party, Republicans, Democrats, Labor, and Business," states:

We the undersigned strongly feel the need for

> **". . . To set the tone of discourse in Congress 2017, we ask that you restate your support for a Glass-Steagall Act during your State of the Union address."**
>
> *Ohio Democrats,*
> *'Our Revolution'*

We applaud your campaign statement in Charlotte, North Carolina, October 26, 2016, endorsing a call for "A 21st Century version of Glass-Steagall" and reintroducing a modern day Glass-Steagall Act. We trust that you understand that stabilizing the business climate and securing the assets as separate from Wall Street speculation is a key to prosperity during your administration.

To set the tone of discourse in Congress 2017, we ask that you restate your support for a Glass-Steagall Act during your State of the Union address.

Be assured in doing so, you will find common ground with both the Republicans and the Democrats since both party platforms have the support of banking legislation that separates insured accounts from Wall Street speculation in their respective platforms....

This Ohio initiative follows on the heels of earlier action by the Illinois House of Delegates which adopted a resolution to the U.S. Congress, not only for

Glass-Steagall, but for a broader program to save the economy. That resolution is given here in part:

WHEREAS, A return to a durable recovery will require adoption of national credit and national banking policies as was done by Alexander Hamilton, John Quincy Adams, Abraham Lincoln, Franklin D. Roosevelt, Dwight Eisenhower, and John F. Kennedy; the program of federal credit to industry, states and cities built the industry and agriculture of our nation;

WHEREAS, National credit, under this Constitutional program, can be made available for the creation of productive jobs in infrastructure, manufacturing, and high technology projects, thus creating mass employment for our now heavily unemployed and underemployed workforce, especially young people; therefore, be it

RESOLVED, we urge the United States Congress to immediately adopt the "American Recovery" program by doing the following:

1) Restore the provisions of the Glass-Steagall Act, and pass the relevant bill in the U.S. House of Representatives and a bill in the U.S. Senate which aim to immediately restore the separation of investment and commercial banking; Glass-Steagall was law for 66 years; it prevented banking crises like the one experienced in 2008;

2) Return to a national banking and a federal credit system, modeled on the principles of Alexander Hamilton's First Bank of the United States, which built all the infrastructure of the nation for the first 40 years; it was re-instituted as Abraham Lincoln's National Banking-Greenback policy that built everything from railroads to steel mills;...

3) Use the federal credit system to build a modern network of high speed rail, power generating systems, water projects, such as those urgently needed in the Southwest and cities like Flint, Michigan; Chicago; Philadelphia; and

> "... Return to a national banking and a federal credit system, modeled on the principles of Alexander Hamilton's First Bank of the United States, which built all the infrastructure of the nation for the first 40 years; it was re-instituted as Abraham Lincoln's National Banking-Greenback policy that built everything from railroads to steel mills;..."
>
> *Resolution to the U.S. Congress, passed by Illinois House of Delegates*

others nationwide; and other critical programs; and

4) Launch a program to rebuild our space program to put a permanent manned colony on the Moon and explore the solar system, and develop a program to create nuclear fusion, to finally solve the energy needs of the nation and the planet....

Similar resolutions have now been introduced into the Illinois Senate, and the North Carolina House of Delegates.

The Battle Lines, and the Stakes

In a major campaign speech at Charlotte, North Carolina, on Oct. 26, 2016, then candidate Donald Trump issued a forceful call for passage of a "21st Century" Glass-Steagall Act. Subsequently, he defended and reiterated that call. Response from the establishment media outlets has been one of almost violent opposition, including demands that Trump remove Glass-Steagall from the agenda of his incoming administration. The life-and-death battle for Glass-Steagall is now upon us. It is not a fight between the Republican and Democratic parties. On the one side is the growing "cross-party" coalition of forces which LaRouche PAC is determined to lead to victory for Glass-Steagall. In opposition, the Wall Street faction in both parties, including among both Democratic and Republican members of Congress, is fiercely determined to stop the restoration of Glass-Steagall.

This is no mere "economic policy debate." In 2010, a senior American economist who was in an advisory capacity to the Obama Administration, was in the City of London, and had a meeting with a very senior official of the British Foreign and Commonwealth Office. This economist was given a very specific message, with the understanding that it would get back to the United States, and would not only get into the White House, but would be delivered as well to Lyndon LaRouche. The message was, that if the United States moved to reinstate Glass-Steagall, this would be considered a *casus belli* by the British. In other words, it would be considered an act of war, against the British Empire, if the United States were to return to Glass-Steagall.

Two years later, in an interview published in *Rolling Stone* magazine, President Barack Obama forcefully and uncompromisingly stated that Glass-Steagall would never be allowed during his Presidency.

Two things that must be understood from these 2010-2012 events are, first, that the Empire which will go to war against Glass-Steagall is not the nation-state of Great Britain, but rather that financial empire centered in London, an empire which most emphatically encompasses most of present-day Wall Street, i.e., those banking and financial forces who see Glass-Steagall as a dagger aimed at their hearts, one which will end their present-day global power. Second, Barack Obama, the puppet of this London-centered empire, is the same President who has murdered hundreds through his personally-authorized drone attacks, and brutalized countless others. Obama's statements against Glass-Steagall must be taken as deadly threats against Glass-Steagall's proponents.

In each of the past two Congressional sessions, more than one hundred Representatives and Senators have sponsored or co-sponsored bills to restore Glass-Steagall, and in discussions with the LaRouche PAC organizing team on Jan. 3, several members of Congress indicated that they are ready to re-introduce Glass-Steagall legislation again in both Houses of Congress. At the same time, glimmers of an actual bi-partisan approach to rebuilding the American economy were seen in last week's press conference by several anti-free-trade Democratic Representatives, such as Ohio's Marcy Kaptur, Oregon's Peter DeFazio, and Connecticut's Rosa DeLauro (all Glass-Steagall supporters in the last Congress), accompanied by AFL-CIO head Richard Trumka, where they announced that they are prepared to work with President Trump on rewriting NAFTA, and will "give very strong support" for any such endeavor.

Nevertheless, Wall Street's puppets—including both radical "free-market" Republicans as well as the Obama/Hillary Clinton Democratic forces—are mobilizing to defend the global speculative regime. The Democratic National Committee announced that it has hired former Hillary Clinton campaign staffers to beef up its "war room" against the incoming President and to "protect President Obama's legacy," as stated by DNC interim chair Donna Brazile—while Democratic Senate Minority Leader Chuck Schumer of New York made clear to Glass-Steagall advocates last week that he is flatly opposed to Glass-Steagall.

• Given the reality that, in the recent election campaign, the platforms for both the Democratic and Republican parties contained planks endorsing Glass-Steagall;

• given the announced support for Glass-Steagall by President-Elect Trump;

• given the support for Glass-Steagall expressed to the LPAC lobbying team by members of Congress on Jan. 3, and

• given the grass-roots mobilization by ordinary citizens, Democrats, and Republicans alike, now taking place throughout the nation;

It is abundantly clear that adequate forces exist now, at this moment, to accomplish a successful passage of Glass-Steagall. The real issue is one of a willingness to fight through for victory.

In truth, the one hundred-plus members of Congress who signed onto Glass-Steagall legislation during the last several sessions of Congress, did very little to actually fight for it. One complaint often heard from them was, "There is no chance of passing this; we don't have the votes." But, was that response one that was motivated by pessimism—or by fear? In the years since 9/11 and the Patriot Act, and since the 2007-2008 bank bailouts—bailouts which defined the integrity of the Wall Street financial system as a matter of "national security"—the power of the London/Wall Street apparatus over our nation has become frightening. Most Congressmen and most Americans fear to challenge it.

Remember that in February of 1933, one month prior to his inauguration, there was an assassination attempt against Franklin Roosevelt, and following that, during the next twelve months a conspiracy was hatched by leading Wall Street elements to carry out a military coup in the United States, a coup plot which was exposed in Congressional testimony in 1934.

Greater courage is now required. Recognize, however, that much of the hysteria, which we are now seeing in the establishment news media, about what "Trump might do," signals that it is now our enemies who are increasingly afraid. The tables have been turned, and the passage of Glass-Steagall is now on the agenda. This will open the door for both U.S. participation in the Russia-China-BRICS New Paradigm of global economic development as well as the full agenda for progress enunciated by Lyndon LaRouche in his Four Laws. An all-out fight, a total mobilization for Glass-Steagall, now! can win the day.

HONORING THE ALEXANDROV ENSEMBLE

The Beauty of Mankind Will Resound

by Dennis Speed

Jan. 8—Only days after the assassination of Russian Ambassador Karlov in Turkey, and the tragic death—in a plane crash on Dec. 25, 2016—of ninety-two extraordinary Russian citizens, among them sixty-four members of the famed Alexandrov Ensemble of Song and Dance, the United States' Obama Administration threw thirty-five Russian diplomats out of the country. This was said to be in retaliation for interference in the American Presidential

Schiller Institute

Diane Sare conducting New York City Community Chorus Jan. 7 at "Teardrop Memorial."

elections through the alleged "hacking" of Democratic Party computers. (President Vladimir Putin, in "retaliation," invited the children of American diplomats to the Kremlin to celebrate Christmas.)

The Schiller Institute's Helga Zepp-LaRouche wrote a statement of condolence for the Christmas Day tragedy, which was delivered to the Russian Consulate in New York City on Dec. 29. The Institute's chorus also sang the Russian National Anthem there, to underscore the "unity in tragedy" that is desirable between the people of the United States and Russia, at such a moment of extraordinary cultural loss. A recording of their performance, which can be seen here, gleaned over 400,000 views in the first seventy-two hours after it became available, with thousands of comments from Russian speakers expressing their deep appreciation for what the chorus had done. Something more, however, was needed, and the Schiller Institute supplied it.

A "living memorial" was organized quickly, involving the chorus and its supporters, New York City and New Jersey first responders, the families of victims of

9/11, and private citizens who understand the immediate danger of war. The seventy-five year-old alliance of the United States with Russia in the period of World War Two, also known as the "Great Patriotic War," demanded a new, "living memorial" of cultural diplomacy that would permanently reverse the evil antics of the 1946-1991 "Cold War," as well as the attempts to invent a "new Cold War" today. The *Teardrop Memorial* in Bayonne, New Jersey, virtually unknown to most Americans, but in fact essential to Russian-American relations, seemed the natural place to hold the ceremony.

Russia and America in Partnership

Friends and colleagues, we gather today to honor the victims of the devastating crash of the Tupolev-154 that happened two weeks ago. We come together to commemorate 92 passengers including members of world famous Alexandrov Academic Ensemble of Song and Dance; the prominent charity worker and humanitarian worker Dr. Liza Glinka; teams of Russian TV channels: Zvezda, NTV; as well as the crew of the plane.

Our thoughts and prayers are going to the families of the victims. The singers, the dancers, doctors, journalists, pilots and stewards, lived their lives for a purpose, especially the performers who used to cheer up huge audiences, but today we stay silent in their memory.

Today is the Orthodox Christmas Day, and on Christmas Day in every nation, we share life, love, we exchange support; we praise each other, we treat each other as being one family. And it's very symbolic that today we gather to grieve at the Tear-Drop of grief that is very dear to the American people for their loss of 9/11.

Schiller Institute

Pyotr Ilyichov

Mr. Pyotr Ilyichov, First Deputy Permanent Representative of the Russian Federation to the United Nations, was standing at the base of the "Teardrop of Forgiveness Memorial," when he spoke these words on Jan. 7. The memorial had been donated by the nation of Russia to the United States in the aftermath of the horrific attack of Sept. 11, 2001, and the earlier terrorist action against the World Trade Center in February of 1993. He had traveled to the memorial to participate in an (Orthodox) Christmas Day "living memorial" of music, and words of gratitude, for the lives, not only of the dead, but also of the families and friends of the deceased, who would be gathered in church or at home this Christmas Day.

Lt. Tony Giorgio of the New York Police Department, who moderated the event, knew the Alexandrov Ensemble well. As the founder and head of the New York City Police Band, he had traveled to Quebec City for a music conference and competition at which his band and the Alexandrov Ensemble had both performed. As a surprise for the Americans, and on the occasion of the 10th anniversary of 9/11, the Russian singers and instrumentalists had performed "God Bless America," sung by baritone Grigory Osipov. Osipov was one of those killed in the Dec. 25 crash.

In his condolence message issued hours after the crash, Lt. Giorgio, the Director of the NYPD Ceremonial Unit, said "It was a wonderful group of musicians and great ambassadors from Russia. And what this tragedy means for us is heartfelt."

Lt. Giorgio's words, covered by *Russia Today*, cemented an initiative that the Schiller Institute's members had been loosely considering in the aftermath of the extraordinary outpouring of support for unity and peace, shown in the thousands of web comments on their earlier performance at the Russian Consulate.

Just as in the original founding of its New York City Community Chorus in 2014, when the Institute had sought to transcend the futile confrontations between police and demonstrators that had haunted New York City in the aftermath of the death of Eric Garner of Staten Island,—so today, the question was whether there might be something further done to send the message, *"Alle Menschen werden Brüder"* ["all men become brothers"], of Schiller's "Ode To Joy," to the people of Russia as a whole, in a respectful, beautiful way, on behalf of metropolitan New York City, and the United States as a whole.

The fact that Lt. Giorgio's experience of the Alexandrov Ensemble's gift of song had occurred on the occasion of 9/11's tenth anniversary, immediately suggested that the appropriate response, on this occasion, would be to stand in front of the very monument, dedicated by President Vladimir Putin in 2006, that the Russian people had given to America ten years earlier.

Terry Strada, Chairwoman of the "9/11 Families United for Justice Against Terror," spoke and personified what true friendship—*Freundschaft*—can mean between Russia and America, as well as among all people everywhere, even despite tragic loss and death.

Schiller Institute

Lt. Tony Giorgio

Schiller Institute

Terry Strada

Schiller Institute

Diane Sare

The name of Strada's husband, Thomas Strada, who died in the Sept. 11 attack, is etched in stone at the base of the monument.

Today, on behalf of everyone standing here, and the American people, I would like to offer my sincere and heartfelt condolences, for the sudden, tragic and senseless death of your beloved Alexandrov Ensemble, your loved ones, and your fellow citizens.

Rich in history and pride, the Alexandrov Ensemble bolstered the spirits of the deprived soldiers defending the Warsaw Pact, and under President Vladimir Putin continued that tradition of patriot purpose. Their performances would provide a moral balance in difficult times, and on Dec. 25, they were traveling to Syria to lift the spirits of the Russian army during their time away from home.

Everyone here knows your pain, how deep your sorrow goes, and the feeling that you may drown in your tears. Grief like this is both physical and heartbreaking, and that the road to healing is long and difficult. Allow yourself to mourn, to cry and to be sad. Remember those you loved, and lost. Remember the beautiful music they made, and how it felt in your hearts when you heard their songs and the sound of their beautiful instruments: They were a gift from God, and they are gone, too soon....

The impact of her brief remarks, the living voice of

those whose husbands, wives, mothers, fathers, friends and acquaintances never returned home Sept. 11, was profoundly felt. One person wrote: "Everyone who has ever deeply loved someone, knows that the person that we love is never really bound or defined by the personal flaws that we all get to know, that we each have. It's the same way with our country. It's something greater than any of us. It's difficult to, at any particular period of time, ever capture that, except in special circumstances, when we have the privilege to summarize the meaning of our whole history in single, short moments. And that is what you did, in what you said."

Their Legacy Will Live On

"The loss of the chorus was particularly great, because as everyone who sings in a chorus knows, the combination of our voices is greater than each of us individually, or each of us added up as parts. Each and every one of us is going to die. But we hope that mankind will be immortal. If we can each think of ourselves as unique voices in a great chorus which stands across generations and across continents, then the universe will resound with the beauty of mankind," said New York Schiller Institute Chorus Director and Founder Diane Sare, whose group performed the Russian and American national anthems and the Christmas carol *Adeste Fideles* ("O Come, All Ye Faithful"). Sare spoke later that day to members of the LaRouche Political Action Committee, and, during that discussion, she cited a statement from Virginia State Senator Richard Black, which read:

Color guards with Chorus in background, in front of "Teardrop Memorial."

A fond farewell to Russian heroes who died for the cause of peace on December 25, 2016.

I pray for the families of those Russians who perished last Christmas while flying to spread beauty to Syria, a land torn asunder by evil schemes of foreign powers. How appropriate that the renowned Alexandrov Ensemble is honored at this place by the Schiller Institute Chorus singing both the "Star-Spangled Banner" and the Russian national anthem at a wreath-laying for the victims of the air crash. The American and Russian choirs shared a dedication to restoring civility by appealing to the higher intellect. Their legacy will live on.

The Teardrop 9/11 Memorial was a gift that Russia gave Americans to honor the 3,000 Americans slain by al-Qaeda on 9/11. That monument was inscribed "To the struggle against world terrorism." How fitting that we honor men and women who gave their lives in that struggle. Their gifts contributed greatly to peace and harmony among men. This event comes at an historic moment in Russian-American relations; an exciting time of joint commitment to civilization and religious freedom, and the restoration of world peace. I am grateful that Russia stepped forward militarily, carrying the burden of confronting world terrorism, while much of the world chose a darker path.

If there is to be a safe and productive future for the human race, it must mean an abolition of the evil of banality in international relations.

The death of a great artist is a tragedy for all mankind, as civilized societies know. When an entity such as the Alexandrov Ensemble is lost, the true character of every nation is shown in whether it recognizes such a loss as its own. In a time when the dogs of world war can still be unleashed, even in the few weeks' transition to the next Presidency, the elevation of relations among nations above the level of the banal, takes on a strategic significance. Culture and strategy become one. A higher conception of man, shared among nations, can ensure that humanity itself survives even in the worst of times. "I will show you a more excellent way," the artist says.

The new cultural platform that Lyndon and Helga LaRouche have sought to establish among nations, is the necessary precursor to sane, and human, economic relations among the peoples of the World Land-Bridge—including the United States and Russia. Music and poetry are the cultural "machine tools" that allow the human race to transcend tragedy in favor of the immortality of us all—the true, sublime weapons of the war for a higher civilization.

FROM ASHES OF SYRIAN WAR

New Axis of Stability and Development Emerging

by Dean Andromidas

Jan. 9—A potential axis of stability and development is emerging out of the ashes of the Syrian War that will transform the region into a productive and integral part of the Eurasian development zone being created under the leadership of Russia and China through the "One Belt One Road" policy. As a result of the end of the Obama Administration, and the end of the nearly two decades of a policy of regime change and war that began under Bush and was carried forward and expanded under Obama, new hope is being felt throughout the Middle East region. The intention of the incoming Trump Administration to end the policy of regime change, adds to that hope.

A new paradigm is becoming a possibility with the ceasefire agreement initiated by President Vladimir Putin, with the full support of Turkey and backed by Iran. It gives hope for the final settlement of the Syrian war. If the fragile ceasefire holds, it should be followed by talks for a negotiated political solution, to be held in Kazakstan's capital of Astana. Both the ceasefire and the talks exclude the Islamic State of Iraq and the Levant (ISIL) and al-Nusra.

In announcing the ceasefire, Russian President Putin said it was "a development that we all have looked and worked for, for so long," but was still "fragile." He nonetheless said it could lead "to peace talks on the Syrian conflict settlement." Putin added that Russia, Turkey, and Iran will act as guarantors.

The fact that Russia, Turkey, and Iran are now cooperating to bring stability to the region is no doubt creating nightmares for the adherents of a British geopolitical policy that has worked to keep these countries in perpetual conflict, not only for the last 30 years, but since the days when the British Empire always tried to pit Russia and the Ottoman Empire against each other in perpetual conflict.

Ministry of Foreign Affairs of the Russian Federation

From left to right, Iran Foreign Minister Mohammad Javad Zarif, Russian Foreign Minister Sergey Lavrov, and Turkish Foreign Minister Mevlut Cavusoglu, in Moscow, Dec. 20, 2016.

The agreement follows a meeting of Russian, Turkish, and Iranian Foreign Ministers in Moscow on Dec. 20. The progress made at that meeting prompted Russian Foreign Minister Sergei Lavrov to assert that unlike the United Nations and U.S.-backed formats, which have only prolonged the conflict, the Russia, Turkey, and Iran format works.

The ceasefire was later backed by a United Nations Security Council Resolution, and other countries have been invited to join in the process.

"It is important to increase the number of guarantor countries, and we therefore want at this stage to invite our Egyptian colleagues to join these agreements," Lavrov said. "Later, at subsequent stages, we could probably get other key countries with influence on events in Syria involved too—countries such as Saudi Arabia, Qatar, Iraq, and Jordan."

Commenting on these developments, Lyndon H. LaRouche agreed, saying that Putin has assured that the Russia, Turkey, and Iran format is one that could work.

TRT World/youtube

Turkish Deputy Prime Minister Numan Kurtulmus

Slamming Obama While Waiting for Trump

The Turkish government totally rejects Obama's support of the Syrian Kurdish YPG and PYD in the name of fighting ISIS. Both are closely linked to the Turkish Kurdish PKK, which is waging an armed insurgency in Turkey, and Turkey considers all three organizations to be terrorists. It is no coincidence that during the period Obama has been heavily supporting the YPG and PYD, they have moved in the direction of establishing a Kurdish entity in northern Syria, which is totally unacceptable to Turkey and Syria alike.

Now, with the assassination of Russian Ambassador Andrei Karlov, followed by a terrorist attack on New Years Eve killing over 40 people, and another attack in Izmir two days later, Turkish leaders rightfully feel they are under attack for collaborating with Russia and Iran in organizing a ceasefire in Syria.

Hinting at the possible role of western intelligence services in the Istanbul attack, Deputy Turkish Prime Minister Numan Kurtulmus suggested that "foreign intelligence services" could be behind the attack, considering how "professionally" it was carried out. "I am of the opinion that it's not possible for the perpetrator to have carried out such an attack without any support. It seems like a secret service thing. All these things are

being assessed," Kurtulmus told *Hurriyet Daily News* on Jan. 4.

The Istanbul New Year's Eve attacker has been identified as Uzbek national Abdulkadir Masharipov. Although it is believed that he was part of an Uzbek cell of ISIL, this has not yet been fully determined. He is still at large.

Former deputy director of Turkey's National Intelligence Agency (MIT) Cevdet Oner did not dismiss Kurtulmus' assertion of a foreign intelligence service connection. He told *Hurriyet Daily News* that despite ISIL's taking responsibility for the attack, "There are strong doubts that the attacker was an ISIL militant," and that "when you examine ISIL's emergence in the Middle East, it is an open question whether there are possible foreign service connections."

In the same interview, Kurtulmus expressed the hope that relations with the United States would be better under a Trump Administration. "We have a strained relationship with the United States at the moment, but I don't think it will last long. I think this tension will soon be eased," Kurtulmus said.

Kurtulmus also referred to Washington's support for the PYD and its armed wing, the YPG. "Will the United States show its existence in the Middle East through cooperation with terror organizations or through its long-standing ally? I believe the United States will undergo a clear change in its position and will cooperate with a state like Turkey," under Trump, Kurtulmus said.

Taking a defiant stand in the face of these terror attacks, Turkish President Recep Tayyip Erdogan said, "Turkey is under a joint attack from various terror groups. Those who do not know us should read about

Gallipoli and our War of Independence." (Gallipoli was a World War I battle in 1915-16, in which the British were sorely defeated by the Turkish army, one of whose commanders was Kemal Ataturk, founder of the Turkish Republic and leader in its War of Independence.)

On June 5 Erdogan continued, "We were accused of not doing enough to combat Daesh. The games of those who support other terrorist organizations against Daesh have gone to waste. Their aim is not to clear the area of Daesh and other terrorist groups; it is to turn the region into a sea of blood and bullets."

Creating the Crossroads between Africa and Eurasia

If other countries in the region join the Syrian peace initiative proposed by Russia, Turkey, and Iran, it would create a community of nations which could transform the region into its historic destiny of being the crossroads between Eurasia and Africa. China's "One Belt One Road" policy is the perfect political-economic framework to bring this into a reality. It is also at the center of the Schiller Institute's proposal for the reconstruction of Syria. Iran and Turkey both have populations of close to 90 million people, making them among the largest countries and economies in the region.

China's Special Envoy for the Middle East, Xie

Xinhua/Ammar Safarjalani
Xie Xiaoyan, Chinese government Special Envoy to Syria.

Xiaoyan, has been visiting the countries of the region in support of the ceasefire agreement and the proposed Astana peace talks. China is also deeply involved in economic cooperation in the region, especially with Turkey, Iran, and Egypt, and is committed to aiding in the reconstruction of Syria.

Despite being under constant attack, including suffering an attempted military coup last July and the ongoing campaign of terror being waged against it, Turkey continues to build the infrastructure it needs, to become an efficient participant in the New Silk Road. In the past six months, it has inaugurated two key crossings of the Bosporus linking Europe and Asia. These include the world's fourth-longest suspension bridge and an automobile tunnel. They follow the opening of a railway tunnel two years go. Then, last month, Turkey announced the initiation of two more Bosporus tunnels, including a combined railway and automobile tunnel, and a pedestrian and light-vehicle tunnel.

On Jan. 3, Turkish Transportation Minister Arslan announced that Turkey, Azerbaijan, and Georgia will have completed the Baku-Tbilisi-Kars railway by mid-2017. "We will finish the Baku-Tbilisi-Kars railway project in mid-2017 and the railway will go into service," said Arslan, adding that the project will link London with Beijing by opening a southern route of the New Silk Road, which would potentially be faster then the current northern route.

Segment of Baku-Tbilisi-Kars railway under construction.

Baku-Tbilisi-Kars railway

Turkey's rapprochement with Russia has opened the doors to extensive economic cooperation. Work has already begun on the Turkish Stream pipeline between Russia and the European side of Turkey, which will contribute to making Turkey an energy hub of oil and gas between Asia and Europe.

On Jan. 6-7, Turkish Prime Minister Binali Yildirim made an official visit to Iraq, where he and his Iraqi counterpart Haider al-Abadi co-chaired the third meeting of the Turkey-Iraq High-Level Strategic Cooperation Council in Baghdad, which declared that both countries would work for their mutual interests as well as for peace and stability in the region. In addition to security issues, it was agreed that both countries will jointly work on water projects and management of the Euphrates and Tigris rivers.

The key security issues discussed included the fight against ISIL, which Iraq is currently fighting in Mosul, and ending the use of Iraqi territory by the PKK for attacks against Turkey. These issues were also discussed between Yildirim and Iraqi Kurdistan Regional Government President Massoud Barzani. The linking of cooperation in security with economic cooperation and integration, is precisely what Iraq needs after nearly three decades of war and economic isolation.

Iran has welcomed this rapprochement between Turkey and Iraq as represented by this visit. "We welcome the easing of tension and the restoration of friendship relations between Turkey and Iraq," said Ali Akbar Velayati, a senior advisor to Iran's supreme leader Ayatollah Ali Khamenei, on Jan. 8, as quoted by Dogan News Agency.

The reconstruction of Iraq, another potential powerhouse, is essential for the reconstruction of the entire region. China is already deeply involved in Iraq. China's China International United Petroleum & Chemicals Co., Ltd. (UNIPEC) is already the largest purchaser of Iraq's oil, while the China Machinery Engineering Corp. is building a 1 billion dollar 650MW gas-turbine power-station in Basra. The China Development Bank and its Export-Import Bank are financing the building of a 150,000-barrel-a-day oil refinery. China Machinery Engineering Corporation (CMEC) is building a 250 million dollar cement plant which is slated to have a daily output of 6,000 tonnes. These are only the most recent projects.

China is also deeply involved in the reconstruction of Iraq's railway network, with Chinese-built passenger trains now in service there. A high speed rail line between Bagdad and Basra is under discussion.

In December, the state-run Iraqi Republic Railways (IRR) company announced that it intends to build a rail line linking Basra with the Iranian city of Al-Shalamcheh. The planned 32-kilometer extension will not only allow passengers to more easily travel between the two countries, especially during Shia pilgrimage seasons, but will finally link Iraq to Iran's rail network, which in turn is already linked to several New Silk Road railway routes.

The link between Turkey and Iraq had been reopened in 2010, but the Syrian war (the line runs through Syrian territory) and the rise of ISIL in Iraq and Syria, has closed the line one again. Once peace comes, it can quickly be opened

The question on the minds of regional leaders is what will the new Trump Administration do. If it carries through its intentions to give up the regime-change policies of the last twenty years, and cooperates with Russia and the countries of the region, as Trump has said, it will find more than willing partners.

Turkmenistan Emerges into the World Of China's Belt and Road Initiative

by Ramtanu Maitra

Jan. 8—Turkmenistan in Central Asia—in isolation by choice since its emergence in 1991 as an independent nation—has begun to emerge from its cocoon and establish active relationships with its neighbors, and a particularly close relationship with China. Its former isolation had resulting in stagnation in almost every sphere of its socio-political economy. This shift was born of the realization that it was necessary to ensure a beneficial life for the coming generations of Turkmenistanis. It was not entirely a result of the change of leadership in 2006, when Gurbanguly Berdimuhamedov became President. A significant part was played, and is being played by China, through its huge Belt and Road Initiative (BRI), intended to engage the Central Asian nations and many more.

Turkmenistan is still in the process of overcoming its isolationism. The government practiced what was called "positive" (or "permanent") neutrality, a UN-recognized status, for almost 20 years as its sole national policy, but has now begun to pursue new initiatives to build a prosperous Turkmenistan.

These initiatives, nonetheless, have largely remained confined within and around the development of its huge gas reserves and the natural gas trade. Although serious security threats within its borders remain, particularly in the South, where it borders on Afghanistan, a developmental awakening process in the immediate vicinity of Turkmenistan is clearly visible: Pakistan—just beyond Afghanistan to the southeast—has become a major potential beneficiary of China's BRI. China has committed more than $51 billion in developing Pakistan's physical infrastructure in connection with the China-Pakistan Economic Corridor (CPEC). Those investments will trigger

requirements of energy, and Turkmenistan's vast reserves of natural gas will surely be in high demand to meet those requirements.

Connecting with Neighbors

How will the natural gas get to Pakistan? That question has already been answered. The Turkmenistan-Afghanistan-Pakistan-India (TAPI) gas pipeline project, which has been hanging fire for years, would bring to Afghanistan, Pakistan, and India an estimated 90 million standard cubic meters of gas per day from Turkmenistan's Galkynysh gas field in its eastern Mary province. The 1,800 kilometer pipeline will traverse a path almost at right angles to the CPEC—almost 780 kilometers through Afghanistan and about 830 kilometers from west to east through Pakistan, to enter Punjab state, India.

It is easy to see why this project has not yet materialized. For years, the lack of security in the region, Turkmenistan's self-imposed isolation, and the lack of developmental initiatives within Pakistan—perpetuated by its economic weakness and the huge security problem—have kept the project on paper only. In recent

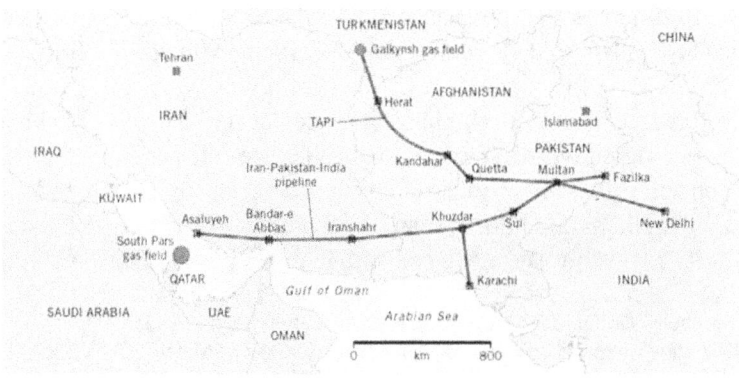

The planned natural gas pipeline, Turkmenistan-Afghanistan-Pakistan-India (TAPI)

months, some baby steps have been taken, but the obstacles continue to overwhelm its execution.

The motivation for Turkmenistan to develop links with neighboring countries is thus clear: It can market its natural gas to China; to Pakistan and India to its Southeast through TAPI; and to the Persian Gulf through Iran. Yet there is another important reason for Turkmenistan to cultivate relations with its neighbors—the problem of the Taliban and Islamic State (Daesh).

Turkmenistan Attentive to SCO

In recent years, activities by the Afghan Taliban along the Afghanistan-Turkmenistan border have caused the Turkmenistan government in Ashgabat to sit up. On the Afghan side, militant groups are seemingly gaining territory:

> For example, the village of Shakh in the Jowzjan province has reportedly fallen to Taliban and Daesh militants, who have institutionalized their position by claiming taxes from the local population. ...
>
> Problematically for Turkmenistan's government, Afghanistan has a significant Turkmen minority, which accounts for three percent of the country's population. Recently, Afghan Turkmen in the Marchak district along Turkmenistan's border have been desperately appealing to the country's political elites for assistance. The area is surrounded on three sides by the Taliban, which has effectively cut the region off from the central government in Kabul; on the fourth side is the Murghab River, and across it, Turkmenistan.[1]

Radio Free Europe analyst Bruce Pannier reported in July 2016 that Turkmenistan's Foreign Minister, Rashid Meredov, made "a rare and little publicized visit to three northwestern Afghan provinces at the end of June." Meredov's trip was the latest evidence that Turkmen authorities are trying to adjust their policies toward their southern neighbor in light of the breakdown in security in northwestern Afghanistan. In dealing with the latest security threat emerging on its southern border, Turkmenistan will have to seek closer cooperation with the Shanghai Cooperation Organization (SCO) and, in effect, with its neighbors. SCO is led by Russia and China and will soon be joined by India and Pakistan. Although Turkmenistan is not a member of the SCO, President Berdimuhamedov took part in its 15th anniversary Heads of State summit in Tashkent last June as a guest, as he has at earlier summits.

Addressing the session, Berdimuhamedov said,

> Cooperation with the SCO is an important component of the foreign policy course of our country aimed at providing stable and balanced regional processes, active economic and trade partnership, and the creation of conditions for realization of large international infrastructure projects. That is why Turkmenistan considers the development of relations with the SCO as in inherent connection with both the advancing course of bilateral cooperation and with the general direction of its participation in regional processes.[2]

Young Nation, Ancient Cultures

The vast majority of Turkmenistan's 5.5 million people—the smallest of the five Central Asian countries—are Sunni Muslims belonging to the Hanafi school within mainstream Islam. Nestorian Christians (properly called the Church of the East) entered the land of today's Turkmenistan in the fourth century A.D.—as they spread widely throughout Asia—but by the beginning of the fourteenth century, lingering traces of Christianity had been completely replaced by Islam.

What is today Turkmenistan was first delineated as the Turkmen Soviet Socialist Republic at the time of the consolidation of the USSR in the 1920s. Parts of the same territory, in the seventh century A.D. for example, formed parts of Khorasan, Khwarezm, Sogdiana, and Tokharistan.

The region is steeped in history. In this land, Alexander's army and the armies of the Roman, Parthian, Persian, and Arab empires, and of the Mongols under Chinggis Khan, and of Timur the Lame, have passed through or held sway. For centuries, a part of today's

---

1. Bradley Jardine, "Turkmenistan's Neutrality Causes Friction among the Ethnic Turkmen Population in Afghanistan," Muftah.org, March 29, 2015, http://muftah.org/turkmenistans-neutrality-causes-friction-among-the-ethnic-turkmen-population-in-afghanistan/#.WHRCCa0z-Wou

2. "Turkmenistan Speaks for Expansion of Capacity Building of World Economic Relations," *Turkmenistan: The Golden Age*, June 24, 2016, http://turkmenistan.gov.tm/_eng/?id=6051

Turkmenistan had formed part of the Persian province of Khorasan, and Khorasan had Merv (next to Mary, the modern city) as its capital. With the explosive expansion of Islam, beginning in the seventh century, ancient Merv became one of the world's greatest cities, known as "the Queen of Cities"; it had already been a stop on the Silk Road for centuries. From Merv, caravans went westward to Iran and Turkey, and eastward to China. Its ruins now stand as silent witness to that glorious and eventful past.

North-South rail corridor from Kazakhstan through Turkmenistan to Iran.

Thousands of years of civilization lie behind what is Turkmenistan today, at archaeological sites such as Kunya-Urgench (on the left bank of the Amu Darya), Dekhistan (a city by the Caspian Sea), Merv, and Old Nissa. The last named, Old Nissa, 15 kilometers west of Turkmenistan's capital, Ashgabat, was the capital of the Parthian kings for 600 years, rivaling Rome itself.[3]

The Driver: Belt and Road

Turkmenistan has a serious land problem: Only five percent of the land is arable (cultivable). The Karakum Desert occupies more than 70 percent (the desert sits atop a vast pool of unexplored gas reserves). The arable land per capita is perhaps less than 0.5 hectares (1.2 acres), but in spite of this, much cotton is grown for export.

Turkmenistan's small population and paucity of currently useful land might be expected to act as hindrance to its emergence as a prosperous and economically significant nation. But its location, and China's push to develop connectivity with nations east, west, and south of the Caspian Sea, could make Turkmenistan a very important ingredient in the future Eurasian land-bridge. At the same time, Turkmenistan is "blessed" with not having direct access to the Ferghana Valley, whose fertile land and density of population of various ethnic groups have attracted Islamic extremists who promote sectarian strife, often exploited by Anglo-American policymakers with the intent to undermine both Russia and China.

Major China-Iran Link

The first cargo train from China to Iran, the "Silk Road train," entered Turkmenistan from Kazakhstan and reached Tehran on February 15, 2016, having travelled 10,399 kilometers with dozens of cargo containers. Welcoming the train at the Tehran Railway Station, Iran's Deputy Minister of Roads and Urbanism, Mohsen Pour-Aqaei, said on that occasion, according to *China Daily,* February 16, 2016:

> To revive the Silk Road Economic Belt, the launch of the train is an important move, since about 700 kilometers of the trip has been done per day.... Compared to the sea voyage of the cargo ships from China's Shanghai city to Iran's Bandar Abbas port city, the travel time of the train was 30 days shorter.

The final link in this north-south rail corridor through Kazakhstan, Turkmenistan, and Iran had been officially inaugurated on December 3, 2014, marking the completion of the Turkmen section of the 908 kilometer route Uzen-Serhetyaka-Bereket-Etrek-Gorgan, which includes 120 kilometers in Kazakhstan and 88 kilometers in Iran. The route, agreed in 2007 and under construction since 2009, opens up a direct rail connection between the three countries to the east of the Caspian Sea. Most of the route is 1,520 mm gauge,

---

3. John D. Grainger, *Rome, Parthia, India: The Violent Emergence of a New World Order, 150-140 BC* (Barnsley, UK: Pen & Sword Books, 2013), "Introduction."

with a break of gauge at the Iranian border. Uzen is connected to Aktau, Kazakhstan, on the Caspian Sea. Aktau is connected by rail to Khorgos on the China-Kazakhstan border.

This route is about 600 kilometers shorter than the more easterly route through Sarakhs, also in Turkmenistan. The new line is expected to facilitate traffic between Central Asia and the Persian Gulf, including shipments of oil and agricultural produce. Large quantities of Kazakh grain are exported to Iran each year.

Galkynysh Gas Field in Turkmenistan.

Natural Gas Hub

Turkmenistan's unique position in Central Asia today centers on its status as a major producer and exporter of natural gas. Turkmenistan exports 44 billion cubic meters (bcm) of the 77 bcm it produces each year. Though Kazakhstan and Uzbekistan are also significant energy producers, Turkmenistan's population of 5.5 million is a much smaller than Kazakhstan's 18 million and Uzbekistan's 30 million, and that reduces its domestic needs and enables a high level of export.

Natural gas from Turkmenistan, Uzbekistan, and Kazakhstan reaches China through the Central Asia-China Gas Pipeline—actually a system of three (and soon four) pipelines. The system starts in the Turkmen-Uzbek border city of Gedaim, runs through Uzbekistan and Kazakhstan, and crosses into China's Xinjiang province at the Chinese-Kazakh border town of Khorgos. The pipeline's length is 1,830 kilometers and its total capacity will reach 55 bcm per year. More than 140 bcm of natural gas was transported to China via the pipeline's A, B, and C lines from late 2009 until March 2016.[4]

---

4. "Gas Supply via Turkmenistan-China Pipeline Increases," *Trend News*, April 23, 2016, which also provides these specifications: Line A and Line B are supplied with 13 bcm per year from the Amu Darya Project in Turkmenistan, and 17 bcm per year from Turkmengaz State Concern. Line C is supplied with 10 bcm, 10 bcm, and 5 bcm per year, respectively, from Turkmenistan, Uzbekistan, and Kazakhstan. Line D, when completed, will receive gas from the Galkynysh Gas Field in

China-Turkmenistan Cooperation

The Galkynysh Gas Field project, which will feed gas into Line D, now under construction, is an example of the close relations that have developed between China and Turkmenistan. (Line D, unlike the first three lines, traverses Turkmenistan, Uzbekistan, Tajikistan, and Kyrghyzstan on its way to China.)

The Galkynysh Gas Field, 75 kilometers southeast of Mary, was discovered in 2006 and is considered the second largest gas reserve in the world. It is actually a cluster of gas fields—South Iolotan, Osman, Minara, and Yashlar—estimated to hold more than 14 trillion cubic meters of gas, and is owned by Turkmengaz State Concern, the state-owned national gas company of Turkmenistan. Gas production began in September 2013.

The first phase of development, requiring an investment of $8.5 billion, was funded through loans provided by the China Development Bank (CDB) and revenues of the owner, Turkmengaz. The second phase, now under consideration, will also be funded by the CDB, and is expected to come online in 2018. China is the most successful foreign investor in Turkmenistan and is the only one that has been given access to a major onshore gas field.

The engineering, procurement, construction, and commissioning contracts for the three treatment plants at the Galkynysh gas field were awarded to Petrofac

---

Turkmenistan.

($3.4 billion), a consortium of LGI and Hyundai Engineering ($1.48 billion), and China National Petroleum Corporation (CNPC, $3.13 billion). Gulf Oil and Gas FZE won a $1.15 billion engineering, procurement, and construction contract to develop the production wells. A boundary security system and terrestrial trunked radio communication system at the project site were provided by Beijing Satellite Science and Technology (BSST), an affiliate of Tri-Tech.[5]

Developing Scientists, Diversifying Industry

Developments in the country and the region, some anchored in the China-led BRI and some stimulated by it, have opened up a new way forward for Turkmenistan. As the country becomes prosperous, increasing diversification of its economic development and fuller utilization of its manpower will take shape. Since President Berdimuhamedov took power in 2006, he has put special emphasis on education and especially science. He is himself a Ph.D. in medical sciences (Moscow) and had a career as a dentist before being appointed minister of health. In 2008, Richard Stone reported in *Science*,

> Among signs of progress, construction has begun on a $35 million building for Turkmen State's physics and mathematics faculty, and a new campus is in the works for Turkmen State Medical Institute. The country is looking beyond its borders as well, with plans this fall to dispatch 1,500 students to overseas universities, including Columbia University. 'If [students] are off-the-charts good, we should do what we can to overcome any obstacles and get them here,' says Peter Lu, a physicist at Harvard University, who lectured in Turkmenistan in 2005. Foreign institutions can play a critical role in the intellectual revival, starting with the next generation.[6]

To diversify its economy and add value to its abundant natural gas reserves, Turkmenistan has made plans to build four plants to convert natural gas to liquid synthetic fuel or gasoline. Construction of the first, a $1.7 billion plant, was launched in August 2014 in Ahal province in central Turkmenistan, based on a framework agreement between Turkmengaz and a consortium that includes Kawasaki Heavy Industries (Japan) and Rönesans Türkmen (Turkey). It will process 1.8 bcm of natural gas per year and will produce 600,000 tons of gasoline. The plant should be commissioned in 2018.

In April 2016, the Ministry of Oil and Gas announced an agreement for the second plant to be built by a consortium including Turkmengaz, LG International, and Hyundai (South Korea), and Itochu (Japan), to convert 3.7 bcm of natural gas per year into liquid synthetic fuels, also in Ahal province. No costs were disclosed or the start date, but the ministry said that it would produce 1.1 million metric tons per year of diesel and 0.4 million metric tons per year of naphtha.[7]

Some efforts are also afoot to develop industrial and consumer products. Turkmenistan is now working with China to establish modern manufacturing facilities with its eye on import substitution and export. A plant for the production and maintenance of equipment for the oil and gas complex is being planned by Merdana Turkmen, a local company, together with the Chinese company, Pekin Sancuan Sencyuri Teknoloji Ko.Ltd. Among the plans of other Chinese companies are the construction of cellulose production enterprises and a plant to manufacture filters for cars, trucks, and agricultural machines. An agreement has also been reached to establish joint facilities for the production of metal products, gas generators, and granite and marble processing.

Turkmenistan is a producer of cotton and silk, and has now engaged China to help in developing its cashmere production. Cashmere is yarn derived from goat's wool. The Turkmen Oguzabat company and the Qinghai Cashmere Industrial Group have agreed to establish a cashmere production facility in Ashgabat using Turkmenistan's raw materials.[8]

These industries, although still nascent, indicate that Turkmenistan has begun a process with immense

5. "Galkynysh Gas Field, Turkmenistan," hydrocarbons-technology. com, consulted Jan. 8, 2017, http://www.hydrocarbons-technology. com/projects/-galkynysh-gas-field-turkmenistan/

6. Richard Stone, "The End of an Intellectual Dark Age?" *Science*, May 23, 2008.

7. "Turkmenistan—Oil and Natural Gas Refining," Turkmenistan Country Commercial Guide, consulted Jan. 8, 2017, https://www. export.gov/article?id=Turkmenistan-Oil-and-Natural-Gas-Refining

8. Huseyn Hasanov, "Turkmenistan, China Negotiating about JV Establishment," Trend News Agency, March 1, 2016, http://en.trend.az/ business/economy/2500810.html

One of the canals feeding the Altyn Asyr artificial lake during construction.

"The lake will solve many problems," according to Paltamed Esenov, director of the National Institute for Deserts, Flora, and Fauna in Ashgabat, as reported in *Science* in 2008. Turkmen officials said that the project would reclaim 450,000 hectares of waterlogged agricultural fields and create a habitat for migratory birds and an inland fishery.[10]

Today, the entire system is functioning and expectations for the project are being fulfilled. President Berdimuhamedov was present at the inauguration of the first stage in 2009, and the system is on its way to becoming a show piece for specialists. According to the state news agency in October 2016, "The implementation of the innovative project of construction of 'Altyn Asyr' Turkmen Lake is a significant contribution to the resolving of global problems related to the conservation of the water resources of the planet." And, one should add, the resolving of water problems has extensive social and economic implications.

Now thought is being given to establishing a center in Ashgabat for promoting the technologies used in the project for further projects in the region and worldwide, and especially for restoring the Aral Sea (Kazakhstan, Uzbekistan) and protecting the Caspian Sea.[11]

potential, since the country is in a perfect position to utilize its revenue from gas sales to develop its physical infrastructure and manpower.

The Golden Age Water Project

Like all Central Asian nations, Turkmenistan is short of water. The shortage of usable water is not only because the Karakum Desert is such a large part of the country. The discharge of drainage water from irrigation systems into natural depressions over many years has caused underflooding (the rise of shallow groundwater levels), waterlogging, salinization of the soil, and pollution of groundwater over an area of 700,000 hectares (1.73 million acres, 37 percent of the arable land). It has also polluted the vital Amu Darya (Amu River).

To overcome this problem, in 2000 Turkmenistan began to plan a $6 billion project to construct two canals that cross much of the country, to collect the drainage water and discharge it into the Karashor ("black salt marsh") Depression, creating a large, new lake, to be called the Altyn Asyr ("Golden Age Lake"), just south of the point at which the boundaries of Turkmenistan, Uzbekistan, and Kazakhstan meet. The depression, 120 by 30 kilometers (75 by 19 miles), reaches a depth of 28 meters below sea level (92 feet).[9]

9. Igor S. Zonn and Andrey G. Kostianoy, "The Turkmen Lake Altyn

Asyr," posted on ResearchGate, January 2013. This is a chapter from the book these writers have edited, *The Turkmen Lake Altyn Asyr and Water Resources in Turkmenistan* (Springer, 2014).

10. Richard Stone, "A New Great Lake—or Dead Sea?" by Richard Stone, *Science*, May 23, 2008, http://science.sciencemag.org/content/320/5879/1002.full?rss=1 This source provides details on the two canals: "For about half its length, the 432-kilometer Dashoguz Collector follows the bed of the ancient Uzboy River. The 720-kilometer Great Turkmen Collector starts in the Lebap region in the east and links up with the Dashoguz Collector 75 kilometers upstream of Karashor."

11. "Turkmenistan's Scientific Approach in Resolving Water-Environmental Tasks: Delegation of specialists travel to the Turkmen Lake Altyn Asyr," State News Agency of Turkmenistan, Oct. 2, 2016, http://science.gov.tm/en/news/20161003news_2016-10-03-1/ and "Turkmen Lake: Water Conservation—A key priority of the environmental policy of Turkmenistan," State News Agency of Turkmenistan, Jan. 5, 2015, http://www.turkmenistan.gov.tm/_eng/?id=4376

II. The New, True Concept of Science

America Must Become Promethean Again! Ignite the Power of Fusion Energy

by Megan Beets

This is Part II in a series on the importance of the Fourth Law, i.e. a Fusion Science Driver Program, of The Four New Laws economic recovery program as presented by Lyndon LaRouche in June, 2014.

> Out of our laboratories may come a discovery as important as the Promethean taming of fire.
>
> —Atomic Energy Commission Chairman Lewis Strauss, 1958

Jan. 9—Did you know that alongside the breathtaking achievements of our 1960s space program, and in the same spirit of optimism for the future of mankind, the United States had a vigorous program to achieve nuclear fusion—the process which fuels the Sun—as a power source, with a commitment to making it happen by the 1990s?[1]

As was obvious during those decades of optimism and growth, the leap to fusion power is not an option for humanity, but a necessity for our continued progress.

By the 1990s, fusion scientists had created gases at temperatures of 500 million degrees (25 times hotter than the center of the Sun), invented new materials and methods to contain and control these gases, and in their experiments had wielded power equivalent to that flowing through the entire nation's energy grid. When the immense powers and potentials of fusion are no longer contained in laboratories, but are widely disseminated through all sectors of human work and life, we will

China's Experimental Advanced Superconducting Tokamak (EAST).

have made a leap upward to an entirely new platform of development.

Today, the potential of controlled fusion stands before us as a breakthrough imminently achievable within the new world paradigm of "win-win" cooperation now emerging under the leadership of China and Russia. For decades, within the now-collapsing paradigm of the trans-Atlantic system, the cynical line has been, "fusion is always 50 years away." Now this lie is falling away, and we stand at the brink of a renewed optimism around mankind's ability to overcome any challenge.

In Part I of this article, "Return to the Road of Infinite Progress: Revive a Crash Program for Fusion Power" published in the Dec. 23, 2016 *EIR*, we covered the elementary principles of creative growth that distinguish man from all beasts, and demand our continuing breakthroughs to more and more energy-dense modes of power (e.g. chemical fuels, to nuclear fission, to fusion).

Here in Part II, we will examine why there is great potential today to organize humanity to conquer fusion, starting with important developments of the past 12

---

1. For more on how the momentum of those early decades was stymied, see "Who Stole Fire from Mankind: The Suppression of Fusion." http://www.21stcenturysciencetech.com/Articles_2014/Suppression_Fusion.pdf

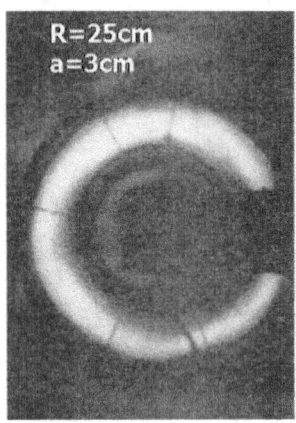
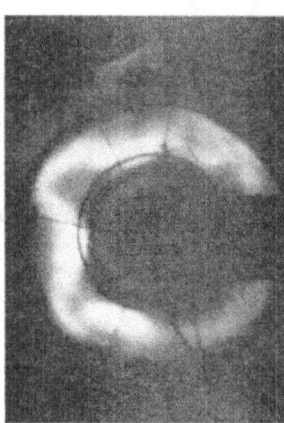

A kink instability, pictured here, can develop in thin plasma columns with strong current along the axis, such as in tokamaks, and other fusion reactor designs. Once they develop, these instabilities quickly disrupt the plasma confinement, and must be controlled.

months in Europe and Asia, as well as the promising recent achievements of the U.S. program, despite its crippled condition.

Fusion Is—and Always Was— An International Affair

As was recognized from the 1950s' beginnings of fusion efforts in the United States, the Soviet Union and Europe, full mastery of the atomic nucleus, put to work for mankind, would not just be a victory for one nation, but would revolutionize our species as a whole, giving it seemingly limitless potential.

The Head of the Indian Atomic Energy Commission, Homi J. Bhabha, who presided over the first international conference on fusion in 1955, said in his presidential address, "I venture to predict that a method will be found for liberating fusion energy in a controlled manner within the next two decades. When that happens the energy problems of the world will have been solved forever, for the fuel will be as plentiful as the heavy hydrogen [deuterium] in the oceans."

There are many challenges to be overcome as we tame the fire of fusion. A fusion reaction is the uniting of two light nuclei (e.g. hydrogen) into one, which results in a tremendous release of energy in the form of electromagnetic radiation and high-energy particles. We can capture that energy to produce electricity, heat for industrial processes, and many other advanced applications, such as rocket propulsion.

In the standard theory, for two nuclei to get close enough to fuse, they must overcome the Coulomb barrier, created by the tendency of two similarly-charged particles (in this case, the positively charged nuclei) to repel one another. This requires a tremendous input of energy. A successful, energy-producing fusion reaction—one which yields more energy than was required to bring it about—requires that the fuel is confined at a high enough density and temperature, and for a sufficient time, such that the energy being given off heats the fuel without further external input. In the process of trying to make this happen, plasma instabilities and other surprising behaviors of the fusion fuel have disobeyed our mathematical formulas, and challenged our assumptions about the characteristics of matter and energy.

Today, stunning new breakthroughs are being made by the impressive fusion efforts which have been developed around the world. If a vigorous crash program of international cooperation were initiated within a new win-win paradigm, we could finally bring to fruition what the old system had placed "always 50 years" beyond our grasp.

Leadership in the EAST

China, which began its fusion program in the 1970s, has developed one of the world's only tokamaks (a type of fusion machine) that uses advanced superconducting magnets, the Experimental Advanced Superconducting Tokamak (EAST) housed at the Institute of Plasma Physics in Hefei. China is the only nation today which is increasing its domestic fusion budget, and it has the intention of graduating 2000 fusion scientists by 2020 (there are currently more than 300 master's and PhD students studying fusion in Chinese universities).

In the recent 12 months, work at the EAST facility has made important progress, and the insights gained from this work can benefit fusion research internationally.

In February 2016, it was announced that with recent upgrades, scientists were able to maintain a plasma in the EAST tokamak at 50 million degrees (over twice the temperature of the Sun's core) for 102 seconds,[2] setting a new record for plasma creation. The goal is to sustain a plasma for 1,000 seconds, at twice the temperature. Professor Luo Guangnan, deputy director of the EAST project, said, "It is a milestone event, a confidence boost for humanity to harness energy from fusion." In November of 2016, another record was set, maintaining a plasma of 50 million degrees for 60 seconds in a "high confinement mode,"[3]

---

2. Being able to maintain the plasma in a steady state is necessary for electricity-generating and industrial applications.

3. High confinement (or H-mode) is a more advanced state of the plasma which is possible to achieve within a tokamak or stellarator, in which the confinement time is significantly enhanced.

National Fusion Research Institute

Korea's KSTAR tokamak with fully superconducting magnets, after a recent upgrade that will allow the study of pulses of up to 300 seconds duration.

nearly double the previous record.

Both of these recent milestones are exciting and necessary advances, and they were not accomplished alone. Scientists in the United States, at General Atomics in San Diego, collaborated with their Chinese colleagues on the experiment, and have even begun operating the tokamak remotely for a "third shift," during the nighttime in China.[4] The cooperation is viewed as very valuable on both sides. "We have made a very good start of international collaboration in fusion research between China and the United States, and we are very proud to be a pioneer in this field," said Dr. Xianzu Gong, of China's Institute of Plasma Physics.

The recent achievements have bolstered confidence to move forward with the next step toward fusion energy, the Chinese Fusion Engineering Test Reactor (CFETR), for which approval is expected in China's next Five Year Plan. This facility would be dedicated to solving the remaining engineering challenges, such as the need for new materials, before moving ahead with a demonstration power plant. The CFETR could come online as early as 2025.

Promising work is emerging in other parts of Asia. For example, in December 2016, a record of 70 seconds of plasma high-density mode operation was achieved in Korea's KSTAR tokamak, breaking its prior record of 55 seconds, set in 2015. KSTAR is the world's only other advanced superconducting tokamak, and began operation in 2008. Major upgrades to KSTAR are planned

over the next few years, intended to allow work that would lead to a demonstration power reactor, KDEMO.

Both of these programs, as others, have been carried out with significant international cooperation, and scientists from all over the world have contributed their work and insights toward this wonderful common effort.

Achievements in the West

Alongside the ongoing disintegration of the system of geopolitics and Wall St. in the west, which has held back scientific progress for decades, glimmers of real optimism appear in the fusion laboratories of Europe and the United States.

At the Max Planck Institute for Plasma Physics in Greifswald, Germany, scientists and students completed the construction of the Wendelstein 7-X, the largest stellarator in the world, in 2014. The stellarator is a design for a fusion machine based on a different concept than the more common tokamak—imagine a twisted tokamak—and may avoid many of the plasma instabilities which challenge the basic tokamak designs.[5]

---

5. The stellarator was first conceived in the 1950s by Lyman Spitzer at what is now the Princeton Plasma Physics Lab (PPPL) in Princeton, NJ. PPPL currently does *not* have a stellarator in operation, though they have a nearly-complete one which awaits a measly $100 million to be assembled and put into operation.

Max Planck Institute

The Wendelstein 7-X experimental stellarator reactor in Greifswald, Germany.

---

4. https://conferences.iaea.org/indico/event/98/session/31/contribution/55.pdf

In February 2016, the Wendelstein 7-X began its experimental operation, and in December released a report that the very complicated geometry of its stellarator is accurate to within 1 part in 100,000. The analysis of Wendelstein 7-X stellarator's geometry was completed with collaboration from the United States and other fusion programs, all of which show great excitement at what can be learned from this unique approach.

Finally, in the United States, though decades of budget cuts have crippled the momentum of a very promising national effort, fusion work has continued in our National Labs and universities, and in recent months has underscored the crime of denying adequate funding to our program.

cc/Bobmumgaard

Alcator C-Mod tokamak at MIT.

On Sept. 30, the last day of its operation due to budget cuts,[6] the Alcator C-Mod tokamak at the Massachusetts Institute of Technology set a new world record, achieving a plasma pressure (one of the key parameters in an energy-producing fusion reaction) of 2 atmospheres, surpassing its own previous record. The Alacator device, a high-magnetic-field compact tokamak, is of a unique design, and could be readily restarted with restoration of funding. Dale Meade, formerly of PPPL, said of the work, "This is a remarkable achievement that highlights the highly successful Alcator C-Mod program... The record plasma pressure validates the high-magnetic-field approach as an attractive path to practical fusion energy."

The Alcator C-Mod is joined in being shut down by the second of three major fusion devices in the United States: the National Spherical Torus Experiment (NSTX-U) at PPPL, which had to stop operations in July 2016, when a magnetic coil shorted out. This leaves the DIII-D tokamak at General Atomics as the only major operational fusion device in the United States. A sane and moral U.S. president would restore funding to the Alcator C-Mod immediately, and mobilize to facilitate rehabilitation of the NSTX-U as quickly as possible.

---

6. "We wouldn't need to invent some fancy new fusion energy or anything..." said Barack Obama, Sept. 13, 2010. Under Obama's administration, funding for fusion was cut again and again, finally forcing the shuttering of many valuable research programs.

Out of necessity, more and more U.S. fusion scientists are turning to international fusion facilities to exercise their talents. Though international cooperation is indispensable, the United States has a deep and revolutionary history in contributions towards conquering fusion, and in the context of joining the new paradigm now emerging in the world, we must immediately restore full funding to our own domestic fusion efforts, that we might maximize humanity's resources in this critical endeavor.

Fusion for All Mankind— On the Earth and Beyond

As the world undergoes a profound and revolutionary realignment, and a new paradigm of "win-win" cooperation begins to take shape, humanity has a renewed opportunity. Nations are being brought together to pursue the common aims of mankind for the mutual benefit of all, supplanting the ideology of the imperial system of globalization which has held back mankind's progress for decades. A vigorous effort to conquer the atom and fully utilize its potential to uplift our species must now be revived as a number one priority.

But these efforts will not take place on Earth alone. The higher potentials of controlled fusion will not see their full manifestation until we go beyond the Earth and begin to industrialize the Moon, and other bodies in our Solar system. Fusion is an indispensable part of an extraterrestrial platform.

In Part III, we will see what the Moon can offer mankind in our mission to wield the powers of fusion.

The Science of Happiness

by Andrea Andromidas

Three hundred years ago, the great thinker Gottfried Wilhelm Leibniz died on November 14, 1716. As he was carried to his grave, his faithful servant Eccard followed the coffin. All the others for whom he had worked, especially the members of the court of Hanover, did not care much. The Prussian Court in Berlin and the Prussian Academy of Sciences also took no notice of the death of their founder and first president.

And yet, only sixty years later, one of the central ideas of Leibniz, the "science of happiness," had acquired such a significance that it was included in the Declaration of Independence of the United States of America: "We hold these truths to be self-evident: that all men are created equal; that they are endowed by their Creator with certain unalienable rights; that among these are life, liberty, and *the pursuit of happiness*."[1]

More than 200 years later, all this has been forgotten. Neither in America nor elsewhere in the Western world does anyone have an idea of what the pursuit of happiness has to do with the constitution of a state, nor what would be understood in Leibniz's sense. Happiness? According to Heidi Klum's definition, this would mean sex, champagne and chocolate, while others might add money or change the order. Because this is so, let us talk about the great significance for the founding fathers of this Leibnizian idea and why they felt that it applies to all the future—including the newly elected President Trump, for example, whether he knows it or not.

Leibniz's Optimism

That the idea of happiness is more than a temporary feeling of well-being is shown by the fact that Leibniz not only spread the concept during the confused period after the Thirty Years' War, but he also connected it to the concept that we live in the best of all possible worlds. Leibniz was born in 1646, two years before the

GOTTFRIED WILHELM LEIBNIZ 1646-1716 DEUTSCHLAND

Wikipedia Commons

end of the Thirty Years' War, amidst the greatest devastation imaginable. After the Peace of Westphalia had finally been achieved, the result seemed rather gloomy: Germany had lost a third of its population, towns and whole lands were heavily marked by the war, science and education had fallen pathetically. Atheistic ideas sprouted like mushrooms and pessimistic conceptions of mankind were commonplace.

But Leibniz was extremely fortunate not to be a child of his time. After the early death of his father, at the age of eight, he was given the key to his library. Thanks to his unusual interest and his extraordinary talent, he was able from this time onwards, in addition to his schoolwork, to become acquainted with the views and arguments of the various philosophers, the old as well as the new, completely unaffected by the tastes of his time. During this time he formed a special, lifelong friendship with Plato. Even before he received his high school diploma and entered the university, he had so appropriated Plato's method of thought that he always responded to the arguments of his contemporaries with this perspective. Among the celebrated contemporaries were some of those still widely quoted today, such as Newton, Locke, Hobbes, and Descartes.

What most provoked Leibniz's contemporaries was his imperturbable optimism. How could this thinker, in a time of the greatest external and internal devastation, be able to assert with full conviction that we lived in the

---

1. From the Declaration of Independence of the United States of America, 1776, see: https://en.wikipedia.org/wiki/United_States_Declaration_of_Independence#Annotated_text_of_the_engrossed_Declaration

best of all possible worlds? How could he assert that happiness is more than a subjective feeling, and that there is even a science of happiness, and that the pursuit of happiness must become the social goal of all men?

I would argue that the concept which underlies these statements seems just as unusual, if not even more alien, to people of our time as it did to people living after the Thirty Years War. The optimism of Leibniz is connected with the conviction that the cognitive capacity of man occupies such an important place in the cosmos that the best of all worlds is inconceivable without it.

This idea seems so strange to our contemporaries, because we live in a time that degrades man more and more. Already in kindergarten it is taught that people consume undue amounts of raw materials, pollute the earth, poison the climate, destroy the planet. It is not unusual to hear the assertion that man is an accident of evolution, that there are already too many of us, especially in Africa, and above all in China, and that in the near future, perhaps after a couple of million years, human beings will vanish once again.

With the degradation of man, the will and the courage for the attainment of knowledge also disappear. Even scientific concepts which were long ago considered mastered are forgotten, buried, or thrown on the scrap heap. One of these devastated areas is economics, which I shall discuss. Regression is passed off as an advance because scientific concepts are replaced by ideologies, esoteric phantasies, untested experiential conclusions, and ever-changing currents of views and opinions, which are appropriately mixed and evaluated according to fashion and are looking for new adherents in daily talkshows in the marketplace of ideas.

There are more than a few who want to escape this confusion, who support ethics commissions for the financial market, moral economics, and equitable coexistence. This also shows the uniqueness of human existence, that at least the longing for truth and justice does not perish in the greatest chaos, even if the path to fulfillment is unclear. Even in Leibniz's lifetime, it was not clear what the good actually was.

Leibniz says, "But since righteousness leads to the good, and wisdom and goodness, which unite to form righteousness, refer to the good, then one will ask what is truly Good. I reply that it is nothing more than what serves the purpose of the perfecting of rational substances."[2]

It must be clearly stated in our era of mental laziness: Leibniz was convinced that there can be no real good without the promotion and perfection of human cognitive ability.

The Establishment of Academies

His lifelong endeavors for the establishment of academies therefore served the purpose of the development of this gift of reason, which finds expression in the perfection of the cognitive capacity of man. Leibniz, with Plato, Nicholas of Cusa, and many others, felt that this capacity of knowledge can not be content with empirical experience alone, and can not refer only to what we see or feel. They were of the opinion that man can do much more, that he must abandon the narrow limits of the sensible world and ascend to the region of knowledge if, as Plato puts it, he wants to look at the eternally existing instead of the becoming, to that which is not subject to chance and opinion, but is of eternal validity. At the time of the Humboldts, a period which was directly influenced by Leibniz' academy movement, this not so easily grasped idea was quite widespread. In his lectures on the cosmos, Humboldt describes how problematic opinions can be when they are only based on empirical observations, or merely spring from feelings:

"From incomplete observations and even more incomplete induction, erroneous views arise on the essence of the forces of nature, views which are embodied, so to speak, in important language forms, and assume the shape of a shared fantasy which spreads throughout all classes of a nation. Next to the scientific kind of physics, another system is formed, a system of untested, partly misunderstood empiricism. Comprised of a few details, this kind of empiricism is all the more presumptuous, as it knows of no facts that might shake its conviction. It is self-contained, unchanging in its axioms, presumptuous like everything that is limited."

On the other hand, according to Humboldt, man, in accord with to his sublime destiny, is called upon "to grasp the spirit of nature which is concealed under the cover of phenomena. In this way, our endeavor extends beyond the narrowness of the sensory world, and we can succeed in grasping Nature, in mastering the raw material of empirical intuition, as it were, through ideas."[3]

2. Leibniz: "Von der Allmacht und Allwissenheit Gottes und der Freiheit des Menschen," 1670, see: http://dokumente.leibnizcentral.de/index.php?id=96

3. Alexander von Humboldt: "Einleitende Betrachtungen über die Verschiedenartigkeit des Naturgenusses und eine wissenschaftliche Ergründung der Weltgesetze." (Vorgetragen am Tage der Eröffnung der Vorlesungen in der großen Halle der Singakademie zu Berlin.) In: *Kosmos. Entwurf einer physischen Weltbeschreibung*, see: http://www.deutschestextarchiv.de/book/view/humboldt_kosmos01_1845?p=22

The Cosmos As Reference Point

In the plan for the founding of an Academy of the Arts and Sciences in Germany, Leibniz at the outset shows that the cosmos of man must be the point of reference: "The knowledge of divine nature can, of course, be taken as nothing other than the true demonstration of its existence. Such must be brought about chiefly by the fact that without it, it is not possible to have a cause (since there is nothing without cause) for why the things which could not be, nevertheless are; and further, why the things that might be confused and confused are present in such a beautiful, ineffable harmony."[4]

The idea of the harmonious, ordered universe, the idea of the best of all worlds, comes from Plato's dialogue *Timaeus*. Because Leibniz gave this idea such central importance in his academy movement, I would like to quote a passage from the *Timaeus*:

"Inasmuch as God wished that all things should be good, and, as much as possible, nothing bad: when he found the visible world not at rest, but rather in unseemly and random motion, he brought it from disorder to an order that appeared far better to him. But the best could never be anything other than the most beautiful; concluding, therefore, according to his nature, with the Visible, he found that nothing that omitted the faculty of thought, as a whole, would ever be more beautiful than one endowed with reason as a whole, which would be impossible unless the soul were blessed with reason. Operating from this conclusion, he gave the soul reason and to the body gave the soul, and formed the universe out of it, so as to complete the most beautiful and best work according to his nature."[5]

Wikipedia Commons

Detail from Raphael's "The School of Athens."

Plato: *Man must abandon the narrow limits of the sensible world and ascend to the region of knowledge*
Aristotle: *From incomplete observations and even more incomplete induction, erroneous views arise on the essence of the forces of nature*

The order of the universe must therefore be the reference point of man. Unlike animals, man can recognize this harmony, never fully, but step by step, in a continuous process of perfection. And he can do more, he can bring his own deeds into harmony with this universe. And because the young United States of America designed its program with this intention, to direct its own deeds according to the order of the universe, the founding fathers wrote into the Declaration of Independence the right to strive for happiness. It does not mean that one will create paradise on earth, but it means that through all storms one is obliged to serve the common good, or in other words, to contribute to the progress of all humanity, even to the development of the entire cosmos.

From this never-ending mission, Gottfried Wilhelm Leibniz drew his imperturbable optimism. His academies and learned societies, as he pursued them from his youth up to the end of his life, were to gather, educate, form, and put into the service of the one human race the entire religious, intellectual, scientific and economic potential of the people, and to further their process of growth and maturity. In a letter to Peter the Great from 1712, he wrote:

"I am going for the benefit of the whole human race, and I am more inclined to achieve something good with the Russians than with the Germans or other Europeans, for my inclination and pleasure go to that which is best for all."

To love God means to promote public well-being and to realize universal harmony, as far as one can contribute to it, "for God has created the rational creatures for no other purpose than to serve as a mirror, wherein His infinite harmony would be reproduced in infinite ways," as he put it in the founding publication of his academy.

This idea was followed by the founding fathers of the

---

4. Leibniz: "Grundriß eines Bedenkens von Aufrichtung einer Sozietät in Deutschland," 1671, see https://leibniz.uni-goettingen.de/files/pdf/Leibniz-Edition-IV-1.pdf, S. 530 ff.

5. Plato, *Timaeus*, see: http://classics.mit.edu/Plato/timaeus.html

United States of America, when, in addition to the right to life and liberty, they also asserted the right to pursue happiness.

Have they ever realized it? Yes, in certain periods, under Presidents Lincoln, Quincy Adams, Franklin Roosevelt, Eisenhower, and Kennedy, whenever the struggle against the influence of the British oligarchy was won—whenever the credit system created by Alexander Hamilton was put into the service of real economic development.

Without fail, when the development of the intellectual abilities of the population became the focus of social life, science and art flourished, and industry made

Eleanor Roosevelt at Works Progress Administration site in Des Moines, Iowa.

extraordinary progress. America had several periods of gigantic ingenuity and growth, one between 1820 and 1830, then between 1860 and 1880, and later still the period of electrification and the space program.

In a manner similar to that of China today, the railway lines, canals, ports and cities, dams and power stations grew. In the cities, public libraries, schools and universities, symphony orchestras and opera houses were built. America became the land of hope for immigrants from all over the world and a catalyst for progress in other parts of the world as well. In these better periods of America, the Leibnizian idea that the wealth and freedom of a country would increase with the mobilization of the creative abilities of its citizens was indeed put into practice. Not for nothing was this America a beacon of hope.

For a New Academy Movement

The America we have known in the twenty-first century to date is not the America which took up the cause of the pursuit of happiness, at least not in the sense that Leibniz understood it. The America we have known in the twenty-first century to date has long lost the mandate of heaven. The greed for the fast money determines the system, and only those who join in without scruple can be full participants. At the heart of all considerations is not the mental capacity and the creativity of the population, but simply Mammon. A collapse of literacy and a wave of drug abuse are spreading, whole industries are rusting, and once great cities

are disintegrating.

The outgoing president waged seven wars, and the devastation there was akin to that of the Thirty Years' War.

But we still live in the best possible of all worlds. And as well, the desire for the pursuit of happiness has not disappeared. The richness of invention is today celebrated at the other end of the world, in Asia. New cities are now emerging there, thousands of kilometers of highways, ports, bridges and space programs are being created. Gottfried Wilhelm Leibniz already recognized 300 years ago that the culture of the Chinese contained this same, universal idea, that the concept of the "mandate of heaven" was nothing other than the "pursuit of happiness."

"I think of heaven as the fatherland, and of all the beneficent people as His fellow-citizens," he wrote in the letter to Tsar Peter the Great cited above.

From all this we can only conclude that we need an academy movement which restores man's capacity for knowledge to its proper place—this time, to enable mankind to strive for happiness.

Finally, a quote from Alexander von Humboldt, from the lectures on his cosmos:

"Man cannot act upon nature, he can not acquire any of her powers, if he does not know the laws of nature according to terms of measure and numbers. Here, too, lies the power of the popular intelligence. It rises and falls with this. Knowledge and understanding are the joy and the justification of humanity."

III. The LaRouche Revolution

EIR will be reprinting earlier papers of Lyndon H. LaRouche, Jr., to familiarize readers with his discoveries.

In Defense of Treasury Secretary Alexander Hamilton

by Lyndon H. LaRouche, Jr.

Note: Lyndon LaRouche was running for the Democratic Presidential nomination in 1987 at the time he wrote this paper. A version of this paper was issued by the LaRouche Democratic Campaign, and another as follows, was published in the July 3, 1987 EIR.

June 22, 1987—Today, Alexander Hamilton, our republic's first Treasury Secretary and Inspector General of our armed forces, seems to be a giant, and our contemporary political leaders Lilliputians by comparison.

When Hamilton entered the post of Treasury Secretary, our nation's indebtedness and economy were in a terrible condition, similar in many ways to the economic disaster we are suffering today. Under Hamilton's program of recovery, our national credit was restored, our banking system became the soundest in the world, and prosperous growth was unleashed throughout most of our nation.

These policies of credit, banking, and economy, which Hamilton outlined in his famous reports to the Congress, became admired and envied worldwide by the name of the "American System of political-economy."

Under the administrations of Thomas Jefferson and James Madison, Treasury Secretary Gallatin scrapped the American System, and introduced Adam Smith's free-trade dogmas instead. The result of this change was a ruinous one. Under Presidents James Monroe and John Quincy Adams, Adam Smith's ruinous ideas were scrapped; Hamilton's American System was restored. National credit, banking, and economy were saved.

Presidents Jackson and van Buren destroyed the American System, and reintroduced the ruinous policies of Adam Smith. The result of Jackson's policies was the terrible Panic of 1837.

I have lived personally through a similar experience in my own lifetime. The Coolidge and Hoover use of Adam Smith's policies, during the 1920s, plunged the world into a Great Depression. Most Americans suffered greatly through 1938, until President Franklin

A parade in New York City celebrates the ratification of the U.S. Constitution in July, 1788, with a parade featuring the ship Hamilton, *named for the chief author of* The Federalist *papers. Under Hamilton's "American System" of economics, the United States entered an era of prosperous growth.*

Roosevelt began his first steps toward preparing us for the war with Hitler he already knew then was inevitable.

Many of you are told today, that it was military spending that pulled the United States out of the depression. I was there, and saw, as did many of my generation, exactly how the economic recovery of 1940-42 was organized. It was not the war which caused the economic recovery. President Roosevelt created the economic recovery to bring the production of our farms and industries up to levels needed to support our mobilization for war. It was not the war which caused the economic recovery; it was the economic recovery which made it possible for us and our allies to win the war.

We could have had an even better economic recovery, if we had not been forced to do this under the costly, inflationary conditions of war. Despite the inflationary costs of full-scale war, the U.S. recovery of 1940-43 was one of the greatest successes in the economic history of the world. All of the prosperity we enjoyed during the 20 years after the war, was a result of the high levels of farming and industrial potential we built up by 1943.

During the past 20 years, under five successive Presidents, our economy has been sliding downhill. Today, for most of our families, local communities, farms, and industries, things are as bad or worse than during the middle of the 1930s. Leading world bankers are warning us that we are near the edge of the biggest financial crash in history.

The time has come, to junk Adam Smith's ruinous policy of free trade, and to return our country to what Secretary Hamilton was first to name "the American System of political-economy." That is what I intend to do as your next elected President of the United States.

Today, more and more political analysts are warning that the AIDS issue will make my presidential candidacy a very strong proposition. When some among these analysts are asked what might be the added effect of a financial crash becoming an issue during the coming months, their eyes roll upward, as if they were about to faint. The response is: "Let us hope that the crash can be postponed until after the 1988 elections."

For technical reasons, the only one who could predict the exact timing of a crash is some powerful government or banking interest, which knew the day on which it intended "to pull the plug." Unless one has that sort of information, it is impossible to predict mathematically the exact timing of a financial crash. However, the international financial bubble is now stretched to the point it is ready to burst. Under these conditions, any significant disturbance could set off a chain-reaction collapse in markets. Anyone who imagines that it could be postponed to beyond President Reagan's January 1989 farewell address to the nation, without the kinds of sweeping changes in emergency policies I would propose, is dreaming wishful dreams.

Therefore, any American who is looking a few months or more ahead, ought to be very concerned with knowing my economics philosophy and plans for emergency action.

My policies are documented at considerable length in a number of published texts, including a special report I presented to the Reagan administration in August 1982, and a follow-up special report submitted a year later. Given the reading habits of most of my fellow-citizens today, it is indispensable that I summarize this topic in a series of shorter articles. In this article, I concentrate on what might be the first question which comes to the mind of the concerned citizen: What is the kernel of my philosophy of economics?

By profession, I am primarily an economist, and, by scientific standards, a very successful one. All of my work in this field lies within the policy-framework of the American System, as defined by such leading economists as Benjamin Franklin, Hamilton, the two Careys, and Friedrich List.

Within that context, I have added an important discovery. My discovery, known around the world today as the LaRouche-Riemann method, does not overturn anything proposed by Hamilton's famous 1791 "Report on the Subject of Manufactures," but only strengthens Hamilton's policies rather significantly. Within Hamilton's "Report on the Subject of Manufactures," the following passage appears prominently:

> To cherish and stimulate the activity of the human mind, by multiplying the objects of enterprise, is not among the least considerable of the expedients, by which the wealth of a nation may be promoted.

The connection between inventions of the mind, and the increase of the physical productive powers of labor, is the kernel of the American System. What I have accomplished, is to show that it is possible to predict mathematically the rates of increased physical-economic growth which will result from an effective use of a specific sort of mental production of a new technology. On this basis, I have been able to provide a new, stronger scientific proof for the reasons that Hamilton's American System promotes depression-free economic growth, and why Adam Smith's doctrine must always lead a nation to new disasters.

Most of the argument in the following pages belongs within the scope of what most readers will probably call "intelligent common sense." Part is somewhat technical, although I am able to describe this in terms which require no mathematics education beyond the high-school level. I make no apologies for including this technical material. Contrary to the apparent beliefs of President Ronald Reagan, economics is a science, which only bunglers would approach with nothing more than a few handy slogans.

By the end of this article, the reader will recognize the practical importance of the technical matters I introduce in the following section.

The Core of My Argument

The fault of most modern economists, and our government officials reporting on the economy, is that these fellows simply do not know what it is they ought to be measuring.

Certain things have been growing in our economy; some things have not been growing, such as farming, industry, stability of banks, and the average standard of living of family households. That which pleases the Reagan administration, it measures; that which does not please the administration, it either does not measure at all, or measures in an incompetent way. As a result, while the economy has been collapsing, the administration has been reporting "economic growth." Hoover promised a "chicken in every pot," but ignored the question: How many Americans would still be able to afford a pot? What is it that we should measure? I summarize the most fundamental features of the problem. Modern anthropologists insist that the earliest form of society was what they term "a hunting-and-gathering society," in which mankind's existence depends upon hunting fish and animals or gathering wild fruits and vegetables. Let us assume, for the sake of argument, that these anthropologists were correct. Look at such a society through the eyes of the economist.

An average of approximately 10 square kilometers of the Earth's land-area would be needed to sustain the nutrition of an average individual in such a society. This would mean that the human population, worldwide, could not have exceeded about 10 million individuals. It would be a very miserable existence. The average

life-expectancy would be well below 20 years of age, and the cultural level a brutish one.

Over a period longer than the past 2,000 years, we have fairly good knowledge of the population-densities and technologies used in major portions of the world. Our knowledge becomes more precise since the great census taken by Charlemagne, especially in Western Europe, where Church statistics are most helpful, in enabling us to estimate population-densities by area with considerable precision. Since the 15th century, the quality of our data is highly reliable for estimating the rates of change in population-densities.

For our purposes here, it is not necessary for me to go into detail on the kinds of methods we use to estimate populations and to cross-check those estimates. The point I am making is a fairly obvious one: a very crucial difference between the behavior of mankind and beasts, as seen through the eyes of the economist.

Today, there are more than 5 billion persons. Even with existing technologies, as the case of Belgium illustrates the general point, we could sustain three or more times the present levels of population, at a standard of living comparable to that in Western Europe and North America during the happier days of the early 1970s. In other words, "since the hunting-and-gathering society," we have increased mankind's potential population by about a thousand times. We have also increased potential life-expectancies by about four times. If we measure all forms of income in kilocalories consumed, we have raised the potential standard of living by much more than a thousand times.

In mathematics, it is conventional to speak of an increase by a factor of 10, as an increase of one order of magnitude. Through technological progress, mankind has increased its potential by about three orders of magnitude. The smartest species of beast could not increase its potential population-density by even a significant fraction of one order of magnitude.

From the standpoint of the economist, the thing about human existence which sets us above the beasts, is that we are able to effect successive advances in what we call scientific and technological knowledge, and are able to transmit that knowledge to one another in such a way as to raise the standard of living of the average person, while also increasing the potential size of the human population sustained at this improved level. No beast's mind can generate or transmit scientific and technological progress.

The most important fact in economic history, is society's power to increase productivity through generating technological progress, and assimilating these technological advances into daily practice of the society generally.

Let us set up a very crude sort of equation, which expresses what we have just said:

$$y = F(x)$$

in which y signifies a rate of increase in productivity, and x signifies a rate of increase of technological progress. $F(x)$ signifies a function expressed in terms of rate of increase of technological progress. Is it possible to construct a mathematical function of the required form? The search for such a mathematical-economics function has been ongoing since the founding of modern economic science, by Gottfried Leibniz, during his work over the period 1672-1716.

What Leibniz did, in this connection, was to establish economic science as a branch of physical science. This economic science was known during the 18th century, into the 19th, as the science of "physical economy." It was sometimes also identified by other terms, including "science of technology," and, in French, "polytechnique." This branch of economics, "physical economy," is the area within which the greatest part of my own professional work lies.

A mathematical-economics function of this sort is possible. My principal contribution to economic science, since my initial such discoveries during 1952, has been to show how such a function must be defined.

This mathematical function can not be solved through use of the methods upon which present-day econometric forecasting is based. Those methods are based on the combined influence of several influential figures of the 1930s and 1940s: Harvard's Professor Wassily Leontief, the principal designer of the present U. S. national income-accounting system, Prof. John von Neumann, and Prof. Norbert Wiener's doctrine of "information theory." These defective methods are known among specialists as methods of solution of "simultaneous linear inequalities." No system of linear inequalities can represent the relationship between rates of advance in technology and rates of increase of physical productivity.

What I did, starting by attacking this fallacy in the arguments of Leontief, von Neumann, and Wiener, was to return to the starting-point of my adolescent studies of Leibniz's work. On that basis, over the course of several years' work, I redefined the problem. My next difficulty was to select a choice of mathematics suited for solving problems of the type I had defined. I found the solution in the work of a leading 19th-century physicist, Prof. Bernhard Riemann. For that reason, my discovery is known as the LaRouche-Riemann method.

The first crucial problem we encounter in seeking to construct the desired kind of mathematical function, is the problem of defining what we should mean by human "creativity" in mathematical language. "Creation" is a conception which can not be represented in any system of deductive mathematics. My adolescent wrestling with the famous *Critiques* of Immanuel Kant, enabled me to understand this problem, where Leontief, von Neumann, and Wiener, among others, had failed to do so.

Define the word "creation." Try it in theology. Try it in cosmogony. What do you mean by that word? Most of you mean, that in one moment, something does not exist, but in the next moment it does. The transition from the first to second moment, you will name "creation." What happens in between those two moments, which causes the new thing to be created? No matter how long you attack that question with the methods of formal, Aristotelian logic, or modern deductive mathematics, you will end up no better than at the beginning. To the person who relies only upon deductive logic, it would seem that "creation" is a word we use to identify something the human mind could never grasp.

That was the argument of Immanuel Kant, throughout his *Critiques*. Kant insisted throughout these *Critiques*,. but especially in his last, his *Critique of Judgment*, that the mental processes by which human beings create a valid scientific discovery, are not intelligible. This was the same standpoint which von Neumann took, not only in his doctrines on mathematical economics, but his mathematical theory generally. This was Norbert Wiener's standpoint in "information theory."

The solution to this problem of mathematics was first shown to exist by a person who was probably the greatest genius of the past 600 years, Cardinal Nicolaus of Cusa. In addition to being the Papacy's outstanding thinker of the Italian Renaissance period, Cusa was the founder of the methods of modern physical science, and the most direct influence on the work of Leonardo da Vinci and Johannes Kepler, among others, as well as a leading indirect influence on Huyghens and Leibniz, among others. Cusa showed how "creation" could be represented as an intelligible idea, capable of mathematical representation.

Cusa was the founder of one of the two leading branches of all modern physical science. Galileo, Descartes, and Newton are typical of methods of formal deduction, based upon Euclid's *Elements*. Cusa, Leonardo, Kepler, Leibniz, Gauss, and Riemann, are among the leading names in an opposing faction in science, whose method is based on a non-Euclidean geometry. By "non-Euclidean geometry," I mean one based entirely on construction, with no axioms, from which use of deductive reasoning is prohibited.

Without going into the detailed history of this scientific issue, it is enough to say the following. Cusa solved the problem left unsolved by Archimedes, the so-called problem of showing why the attempt at a simple squaring of the circle is based upon a mistaken assumption. Cusa discovered a geometrical and physical principle, which he defined as the "Maximum Mininum" principle, which modern mathematicians know in the guise of "the isoperimetric theorem" of geometric topology. The greatest advance beyond Cusa's original formulation, was contributed by Karl Gauss. A number of Gauss's contemporaries and collaborators worked on refining Gauss's discovery. The results of this were summed up in the work of Riemann.

Today, we call the variety of mathematical physics based on Gauss's approach to constructive geometry "the Gauss-Riemann complex domain." Riemannian physics is based, centrally, on the mathematical representation of processes which evolve to higher states. This is the only branch of mathematical physics in which it is possible to account for what occurs during that interval, constituting the act of creation, between the two moments of successive not-being and being.

This is not the place to elaborate this significance of "Riemann surface functions." Our purpose here, is simply to identify the nature of the problem of representation, and the location in which the required form of mathematical solution is to be found. The following points must, however, be made.

If you imagine that the only self-evident form of action in the universe were circular action, as Cusa showed, then all of the true theorems and constructions in Euclidean geometry can be developed, in a non-deductive, non-Euclidean way, by construction. This is done, first, by imagining the case in which circular action is acting upon circular action, as if the one is at right angles to another, and that this is occurring at every interval of each circular action. This is called doubly-connected circular action. Euclidean space, elaborated by rigorous methods of non-deductive (non-Euclidean) construction, is essentially triply-connected.

With Gauss, we go a step further. We know that simply circular action is not an adequate representation of the real universe. Imagine a special form of circular action, in which the radius of rotation is lengthening as the action occurs: spiral action. Now, imagine that the center of rotation is moving forward, in the direction of time, while this is occurring. Our spiral action now lies on the exterior surface of a cone. This is called a self-similar spiral, for obvious reasons. Now, in place of circular forms of multiply-connected action, substitute multiply-connected self-similar-spiral action.

State what you have done in the language of trigonometry, using elliptic, hyperbolic, and hyperspherical trigonometric functions to accomplish this result. The result is the Gaussian form of the complex domain. It is the Riemannian form of this Gaussian complex domain, which permits us to represent those kinds of processes which are properly called "creative."

Although this Riemannian approach implicitly permits us to map brain functions in a broad way, the LaRouche-Riemann method considers only one aspect of these brain functions, the problem of representing the generation of higher-order technologies. Admittedly, at first glance, what we are able to accomplish in this way is "mind-boggling," but after becoming used to the ideas involved, it all seems quite obvious.

Beginning with a set of three scientific papers which Riemann composed, during 1853, as the dissertations qualifying him for inauguration as professor at Gauss's Göttingen university, the central feature of Riemann's work as a whole is his concentration on the hypothesis, that any physical process in the universe was mathematically representable in the Gaussian complex domain. Riemann supplied only partial proofs for this, but he made substantial advances, and pointed the way in the direction in which more general proofs might be developed. What he did accomplish, is more than sufficient for the needs of the economist.

Referring to the function, $y = F(x)$, our first problem is that of defining the way in which both y, a rate of increase of productivity, and x, a rate of increase of technological progress, must be measured. The problem of defining y, is the simpler part of the task. Defining x is the major challenge. It is that major challenge we are addressing at this point.

If we can represent efficiently any physical process which represents a new technology, part of the problem of defining x is already solved. If we can also define which kinds of physical processes are more advanced, and show that in the same way we represent particular physical processes, we can measure which process is the more advanced technology. We can also measure how much more advanced it is. How do we compare two physical processes, and say that one is measurably superior economically to another?

Go back to the work of Leibniz, where this problem was first defined.

Leibniz's major work in economic science began in Paris during the same years, 1672-76, he solved Kepler's plan for creating a differential calculus. His work in Paris, together with that of Christian Huyghens, was done under the sponsorship of the French minister Jean-Baptiste Colbert. The mission in which Huyghens and Liebniz were involved then, was to design what became known as "the industrial revolution." Leibniz defined this task as study of the principles of the use of heat-powered machinery, by means of which "one man can do the work of a hundred."

This involved the principles of design of heat-powered machinery. Huyghens worked, for example, upon what became known later as the piston-powered internal combustion engine. Leibniz's work led him to collaborate with Denis Papin in the creation of what became the first steam engine successfully used to power a boat (using external combustion).

The general problem at the center of Leibniz's work in economics, was to define the way in which increasing the amount of coal-burning power supplied to a machine, would increase the productive power of the operator of the machine. It is generally true, that increasing the power used per operative will make possible increases of the productivity of the operative. It is also true, that by raising the operating temperature of processes, we can not only increase the productivity of the operative, but can perform kinds of work which are impossible to accomplish economically at lower temperatures.

However, Leibniz's work took him beyond these problems. I shall describe the deeper problem in the simplest possible terms of illustration. Imagine that two machines use up the same amount of heat per hour, and that both are used to do the same kind of work, but, that the same operative, using one machine, will produce more than with the other machine. Assuming that both machines are well built, according to their design, how should we define the difference between these two machines?

Leibniz called this difference "technology." By "technology," we mean, broadly speaking, the quality

Were Alexander Hamilton alive today, he would smile as he accused me of "stealing his program." Then, he would ask, "Show me how you worked out the methods for measuring the connection between rates of technological progress and rates of increase of productive powers of labor." We wouldn't talk about much else, since on everything else we would agree automatically.

of organization of the machine's design. One of the simplest examples of this notion of "organization," is the use of a sharper and harder point, or cutting-edge on a tool. The same work can be done with less effort, and usually better. We develop a more general notion of organization, by defining all machine functions in terms of rotary motion.

What we desire to know, is some principle of organization of machine design, which enables us to predict what kinds of changes in internal organization of the machine represent a more effective way of converting heat-power into increased productivity of the machine's operative. This principle permits us to measure the superior organization of one machine over another. This measurement is the measure of quantity called "technology. "

To keep the discussion as short as possible, let us define rotary motion in terms of what Leibniz defined as physical least action. Most of the preliminary work on defining principles of technology was undertaken by Lazare Carnot and Gaspard Monge's circles at France's Ecole Polytechnique, with the fundamental work established during the years 1794-1815, before the Ecole began to decay under the post-1815 leadership of Laplace and Cauchy. Most of the basic principles of technology of design of heat-powered mechanical devices were solved by the Ecole during that period or soon after.

These collaborators of Carnot and Monge went further, to begin to define some of the problems of electrodynamics in particular, as well as thermodynamics in general. The work of Sadi Carnot, Fourier, and Legendre is the most important. However, as French scientists were repressed under the regime of Cauchy, the world's leadership in scientific progress began to shift into Prussia as early as the 1820s, with one center at Berlin, under the leadership of Alexander von Humboldt, and another around Gauss at Göttingen. During the 1820s, Gauss and his collaborator Weber, undertook a comprehensive reworking of electrodynamics. During the 1850s, this work on electrodynamics accelerated, centered in the collaboration between Riemann and Weber.

As briefly as possible, now. There is a grave flaw of inadequacy in Fourier Analysis. The combined work of Gauss, Weber, Dirichlet, Riemann, Weierstrass, and Cantor, was focused upon this problem of Fourier Analysis to a large degree. Gauss's complex domain provided a unique basis for correcting this flaw. A more advanced view of hydrodynamics was integrated with electrodynamics. This view permits us to do for the technology of electrodynamics what the Ecole Polytechnique did for the technology of mechanics and simpler thermodynamics.

The key clue is to base a notion of physical least action on multiply-connected self-similar-spiral action, rather than upon multiply-connected circular action. This approach permits us, today, to subsume modern plasma physics and coherent electromagnetic pulses under Leibniz's notion of technology. In the conclusion of this article, I shall indicate the major practical importance of that fact for organizing a long-term U.S. economic recovery today.

All other things being equal, there are three conditions which must be met to generate a generalized advance in productivity of operatives:

An 1837 lithograph published by H. R. Robinson, N.Y.

Presidents Andrew Jackson and Martin van Buren destroyed Hamilton's "American System" economics, and reintroduced the ruinous policies of Adam Smith. The result of Jackson's policies was the Panic of 1837, illustrated in a contemporary cartoon. The drawing shows "Old Hickory" Jackson beating the bankrupt nation.

1. The amount of usable energy supplied, both per capita and per square kilometer, must increase.

2. What is sometimes termed the "effective energy-flux density" of the energy supplied and applied, must increase.

3. The level of technology in internal organization of the process of production, must be advanced.

These three conditions are interdependent. If these conditions are not met, productivity of production will tend to stagnate, and ultimately will collapse.

One other point must be added now, before turning to the problem of proper measurement of productivity itself. The fact that we can represent technological progress mathematically, means that we can represent this in terms of the kinds of mental processes which generate these discoveries. This does not explain everything about the human mind, but it describes what mental processes must do to discover a scientific advance beyond existing levels of technology. To this degree, creativity is rendered intelligible.

To choose what to measure as increase of productivity, takes us back to the illustration given at the begin-

ning of this section. What determines whether a change is for the better of society, or not? The answer should be obvious. Most simply: whatever increases the potential population-density of society, whatever increases the number of persons who can be sustained, in an improved standard of living and culture, per square-kilometer of land-area.

We consider the problem of making such measurements at several successive levels of sophistication.

Since our definition of increased productivity must correspond to increase of potential population-density, we should not measure output in either prices or particular products. We measure output in terms of "market-baskets" of consumers' and producers' requirements. The number and qualities of products in market-baskets changes with technological progress. Labor of a higher quality of productivity requires a higher standard of living to maintain its household at that level of cultural potential. So, we must measure how many individual market-baskets' worth of output are produced by the labor of a single operative. We must take into account both consumers' market-basket requirements, and producers' requirements measured in the same way.

The Corliss steam engine at the 1876 centennial exposition. With the reintroduction of American System methods after the Civil War, such inventions spurred unprecedented industrial growth.

The problem of diminishing returns on natural resources comes into play. Here, energy comes directly into play. The more energy per capita, and the greater the effective energy-flux density of that energy, the poorer the quality of natural resources we can use without suffering an increase in cost of production. As we are able to use poorer natural resources economically, the limits of natural resources are widened; whereas, if we do not advance technologically, the limits of natural resources close in upon us.

If we are broadening the limits of natural resources, the result is that an average square kilometer of land will sustain an increasing number of people. If our technological progress is stagnant, the limits of natural resources are closing in upon us. If we slip backward technologically, and have less energy used in production, per capita and per square kilometer, the society is on the road to collapse.

For these reasons, it is not adequate to measure productivity in terms of present-day market-baskets. What we must measure is a rate of increase of productivity, a rate which must be high enough so that we are broadening the limits of natural resources, rather than allowing them to close in upon us.

Political-Economy

A modern economy has two interdependent aspects. The first aspect, which we have stressed so far, is the physical economy: the production and physical distribution of goods. This is the aspect of the economic process which falls under the heading of physical science, as we have reviewed what is involved in that. The second part is the political processes governing an economy. These political processes include the issuance of money, the organization of credit and banking, taxation, and tariffs.

Since employment, production, and physical distribution, on the real, or physical side of the economic process, are organized through buying and selling at money-prices, and are fostered or suppressed by the way credit and banking are organized, and are affected by taxation, the two sides, the physical and political, interact in this way. This interaction is what we ought to understand one another to mean when we use the term "political-economy."

Our Founding Fathers' knowledge of physical economy was obtained, from about 1766, in the relatively greater degree from French industry and science, and their theoretical knowledge from Leibniz or Leibniz's indirect influence. The emphasis on "productive powers of labor" in Hamilton's "Report on the Subject of Manufactures" is strictly Leibnizian. Their notions of the political side of the economic process are best traced to the pre-Andros period of the Massachusetts Bay Colony, and the 18th-century influence of Cotton Mather. Benjamin Franklin's 1729 "A Modest Inquiry into the Nature and Necessity of Paper Money," is an affirmation of Cotton Mather's policy, a policy based on the successful use of paper money issue and "state banking" in the pre-Andros Massachusetts Bay Colony.

Our Founding Fathers had none of the illusions about "the magic of money" popular around Washington-and elsewhere—today. They knew that the source of wealth was the production of physical goods and of public improvements such as roads, canals, bridges, ports, and similar works. Paper money, credit, banking, and so forth, were necessary arrangements for efficient commerce, but nothing more than that.

Today, when I outline what I shall do as President, someone always pops up to ask, "Where is the money coming from?" Very simply, under our Constitution, the U.S. Congress shall enact a law, authorizing the issuance of between $500 billion and $1 trillion of U.S. Treasury currency-notes. This money will not be spent by the federal government. It will be lent, through banking-system channels, to farmers, manufacturers, public utilities, and capital accounts of federal, state, and local agencies responsible for building public works. We shall put farms, industries, and people back to work producing new physical wealth. They will produce more wealth than is loaned to get this production into motion. Their wages, and the business income of farms and industries, will put added money into circulation, increase the tax-revenues of the federal government (without raising tax-rates).

If this money is loaned at low borrowing-costs, at prime rates less than 2%, and if federal tax schedules provide generous investment tax-credits to those who invest in creating high-technology work-places in production, we shall do quite well without having to borrow money from anyone but ourselves.

The problem today, and over the past 20 years, has been, that the political side of the economy has been mismanaged, very badly. The percentage of the total labor force employed in producing physical wealth has been collapsing, while the combined total of unemployment, and employment in administration and superfluous services has piled up. Tremendous fortunes have been made in pure financial speculation, with no increase of physical production to show for it. We have been going deeper and deeper into debt, to produce less and less per capita. It's a terrible way to run a railroad.

The only major risks in the government's creating very large issues of money for lending are that the lending and tax policies might move money in the wrong direction—into more financial speculation, and more and more employment in administration and marginal qualities of services. The trick is to lessen the tax burden on investments in high-technology, goods-producing work-places, and to steer most of the newly created credit into those kinds of investments.

My immediate goal is to add 5 million new industrial work-places, emphasizing improved technologies, during the first two to three years of my administration, and steer the nation in the direction of employing about half of the total national labor force into occupations as farmers, industrial operatives, and operatives employed in constructing and maintaining utilities and public works.

There is no magic in it. It is simply a matter of government reaching a consensus with entrepreneurial farmers and industrialists, and government's delivering on promises to promote technological progress in and expansion of production and employment in manufacturing industries and similar forms of employment. Set the investment tax-incentives high, keep low-cost credit flowing through the private banks, and ensure that there is a sufficient rate of scientific progress being generated.

This program will not be inflationary. It will be deflationary. The higher the percentile of the labor force employed in producing wealth, and the lower the percentile employed in administration and marginal services, the lower the cost of every article produced—the fewer the number of overhead salaries tacked onto the price of what the farmer or industrial operative produces. Keep financial speculation down, too. That will be indispensable under conditions of financial crisis; it is a good practice generally, since every dollar of income from financial speculation becomes an added dollar of overhead tacked onto prices of commodities.

Let us suppose that I were President for two terms. In that case, before I left office, the percentage of our national labor force employed as manufacturing operatives would have doubled, while the number of working farmers would remain about the percentage existing today. This would nearly halve the real cost of every manufactured item produced, simply through large cuts in the overhead burden tacked onto the price of things produced.

Balance the budget? Easily! The trick of balancing the budget, is, essentially, keep tax-rates low and tax-revenues high. How? Simply: Increase national income. Low tax-rates mean, among other things, a more rapid investment in new work-places. By expanding production, the government gains more from expansion of the revenue base, than it loses by not raising tax-rates. Government must strike a reasonable balance between the two, subject to imperative national needs.

The political side of the economy is the easiest part of the problem. We need nothing more than a government with the knowledge, political will, and political support to do what must be done. The real mental challenges come in the area of physical economy.

My 'Science-Driver' Program

My first concern, as President, apart from preventing the financial system from blowing wide open, will be to get rates of productive employment up. Those among you old enough to remember 1940-43, will understand this the quickest. We must begin with the plant facilities and work-places which we can reopen for production. A few years down the line, after new capital investments in plant and machinery take hold, the high rates in technological progress will be seen. That's the way it worked during 1940-43; that is approximately the way it will work during most of my first administration.

It will be during the last two years of my first administration, that the impact of technological progress will begin to be felt by the population more generally.

My duty, is to ensure that long after I am out of office, the United States is absorbing improved technologies at rates sufficient to increase our per capita output tenfold approximately each generation. This is not pie in the sky; we already have, or have in sight, new technologies adequate to trigger the greatest boom in the history of mankind.

I start with scientific and related manpower. To achieve what I have set as my goal, we must build up the percentile of combined scientists, engineers, and research-and-development operatives to about 10% of the total labor force.

My next problem, is to rebuild the U.S. machine-tool industry to a scale and rate of turnover sufficient to transfer the new technologies generated in research and development into production in general. If investment tax-credit incentives are high enough, and if large flows of low-cost credit are flowing into industry, industry's appetite for improved products of the U.S. machine-tool sector will be enormous. Government must ensure that the machine-tool sector is being fed with large doses of the kinds of technological progress which our industries will gobble up under such circumstances.

The President, with cooperation of the Congress, has three major economic weapons for fostering high rates of technological progress: 1) U.S. military expenditures; 2) non-military research and development programs wholly or partially backed by government; and 3) public works, both governmental and by public utilities. If the federal government plans its budgets in these three areas properly, the government can shape the net impact of this expenditure to foster high rates of technological progress spilling over into private investment.

The practical problem on which I have been working for about a decade, most emphatically, is to devise the best way in which either I, or some other President could do this.

It happens that all technological progress likely to occur on Earth during the coming 50 years will be concentrated in four areas:

1. Organized plasma processes at very high energy-flux densities. Controlled thermonuclear fusion as a primary energy source for man on Earth, and in space-exploration, is a leading part of this. However, with these "temperatures," and with associated techniques for handling hot plasmas, every branch of metallurgy will be revolutionized, breaking the limits of every presently imaginable limit to natural resources on Earth.

2. Controlled pulses of coherent electromagnetic radiation, and compound pulses of this sort. This is already emerging as a revolution in machine-tool design, and will be the machine-tool industry of the future.

3. Optical biophysics. A major advance beyond molecular biology is currently in progress, the study of all living processes as characteristically tuned electromagnetic processes of special characteristics. This direction in biology was implicit in the work of Luca Pacioli and Leonardo da Vinci, and was accelerated for a while by the work of Louis Pasteur and others on "optical activity" of living processes. Modern techniques enable us, increasingly, to get at these processes in the very small. A revolution in biology is now in progress as a result.

4. New dimensions in computer technology. We now need urgently what are called "parallel processing" modes of computer design, capable of processing billions or even trillions of "flops" per second. Progress in this direction is under way. Under way, but more distant, is the development of new kinds of optical-analog/digital hybrid computers, capable of performing explicit solutions to nonlinear problems stated in terms of the Gaussian complex domain. We need such instruments for many branches of laboratory and other research. We need such instruments to aid us in remote control of the new, energy-dense productive processes, and in space-exploration applications.

For the next 10 to 15 years, there are three very urgent programs of government, each of which requires intensive investment in some or all of these four areas. 1) Military. Moscow's rapid development of its own version of "SDI," of which the first generation is supposed to be deployed by 1992, and Moscow's rapid progress in developing radio-frequency and other strategic and tactical assault weapons. 2) Biology. It is very unlikely that we shall master a cure for AIDS without a leading contributing role by optical biophysics research. Progress in this direction will also be important in our continuing efforts to conquer cancer, and to deal with various problems of diseases of aging of tissue. 3) A Moon-Mars colonization project, with the objective of establishing the first permanently manned colony on Mars by about 2027 A.D.

I intend to steer as much of the military procurement budget as possible into advanced systems. This will be indispensable to maintain effective national defense, and will have the side-benefit of building up our machine-tool sector, to the great advantage of the civilian sector.

We should probably be spending about $3 billion a year on biological research into a cure for AIDS. A very large fraction of this should go into optical biophysics, including more efficient instruments for detecting various forms of AIDS-like and other viruses in samples. Much of this expenditure will go for laboratory instruments of advanced design, indispensable for this research. This will generate a valuable new branch of industry within the machine-tool sector.

The Moon-Mars program is not an optional "prestige" project. The primary mission of the program is the establishment of astrophysical laboratories at a required distance from the Sun. The principal duty of these installations near the orbit of Mars is to focus upon very unusual phenomena in our own and distant galaxies. The immediate benefit of this, is uncovering new physical principles of the universe, principles which will become indispensable for life on Earth during the second half of the coming century.

Since a sound Mars colonization program will require about 40 or more years to develop, we must begin now, or we may be starting too late for our great-grandchildren's needs.

The only foreseeable way in which we could colonize Mars economically, would be to build much of the spacecraft and equipment we shall use on Mars on the Moon. So, the industrialization of the Moon (largely with automated or semi-automated industries) is a necessary stepping-stone to Mars colonization.

This Moon-Mars program, to be completed step by step, over about 40 years, I project as the main science-driver program of my own and later administrations. In manpower, the project will be approximately the scale the Kennedy administration adopted for the NASA program. The NASA program repaid the U.S. civilian economy with more than 10¢ of benefits for each penny spent on NASA. The Moon-Mars program will have the same kind of effect.

For example, the first step is to develop a cheaper and better way to get into Earth's orbit from Earth's surface. We are at the limit of efficiency and cost for rocket-power. We are now ready to proceed with a better approach. This new approach will be a two-part airplane-rocketship. The aircraft will go high into the stratosphere at speeds between eight and sixteen times the speed of sound. There, the aircraft will launch the rocketcraft, and return to an airport on Earth. I have two designs for such a system on my desk, one developed in West Germany, and a modification of the German program developed in Italy. We are speaking of something which could be developed to fly within about seven years, allowing for all reasonable bottlenecks.

Such a hypersonic aircraft would have other uses. At eight times the speed of sound, we could fly to the most distant airport on Earth in not more than three-and-a-half hours. At double that, we could reach Tokyo in about an hour, and Western Europe in about a half-hour flying time, probably about an hour from terminal to terminal. Developing such aircraft would mean a giant leap in the retooling of our aircraft industry, and in retooling of the firms which are vendors to that industry. The same technologies would have many other uses besides those in aircraft design as such.

The way the Moon-Mars program would pay us back would be in five-year-long half-cycles. We would have to ante up the advance money to cover the entire investment in each five years of the program's phases, but, during the second five years, our economy would be paid back in improved productivity gained from the technologies developed over the preceding five years, and so on. By the time the first permanent colony was established on Mars, the entire project would not have cost us a net cent; we would have made a substantial profit on the entire investment.

These various research and development programs would be the government's contribution to generating the new technologies needed to push the development of the machine-tool sector, and thus ensure that the private sector had the highest possible rate of technological progress, and increases in productivity.

To ensure the best result, the Departments of Treasury, Commerce, and Energy would make use of the LaRouche-Riemann method. That method of analysis would be used to monitor bottlenecks in the flow of advanced technologies into the economy, to detect the problem; and work to correct it long before any significant slowing of the rate of national economic growth occurred.

Were Alexander Hamilton alive today, he would smile as he accused me of "stealing his program." Then, he would ask, "Show me how you worked out the methods for measuring the connection between rates of technological progress and rates of increase of productive powers of labor." We wouldn't talk about much else, since on everything else we would agree automatically.

www.ingramcontent.com/pod-product-compliance
Lightning Source LLC
Chambersburg PA
CBHW080834310526
45788CB00020B/3563